A TREASURY OF XXth CENTURY MURDER

Famous Players

NBM
ComicsLit

cloth: ISBN: 978-1-56163-555-9
paperback: ISBN: 978-1-56163-559-7
Junior Library Guild Edition: ISBN: 978-1-56163-560-3
©2009 Rick Geary
Printed in China

5   4   3   2   1

Comicslit is an imprint
and trademark of

NANTIER · BEALL · MINOUSTCHINE
Publishing inc.
new york

FAMOUS PLAYERS

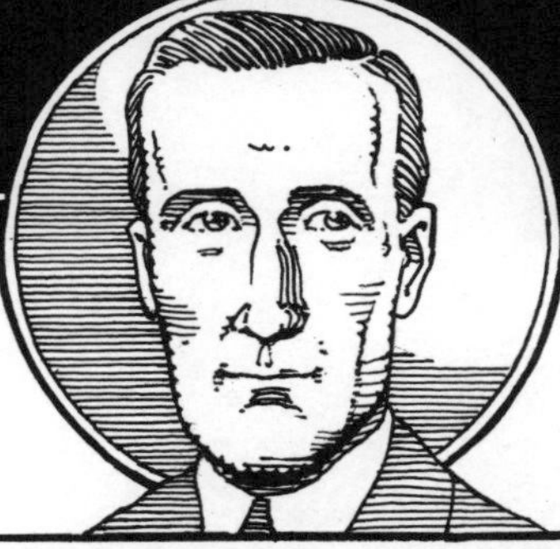

THE MYSTERIOUS DEATH OF WILLIAM DESMOND TAYLOR

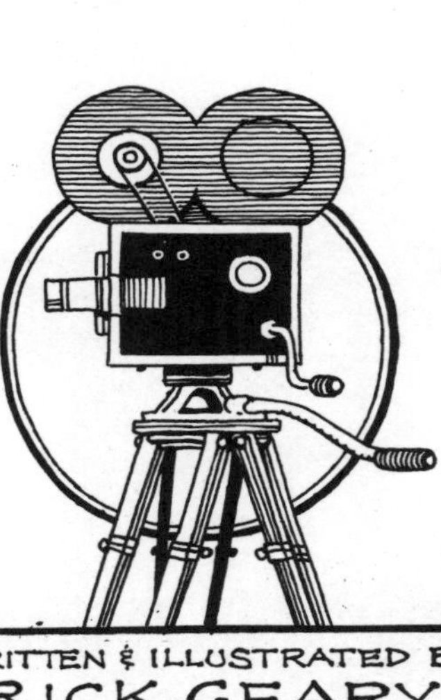

WRITTEN & ILLUSTRATED BY
RICK GEARY

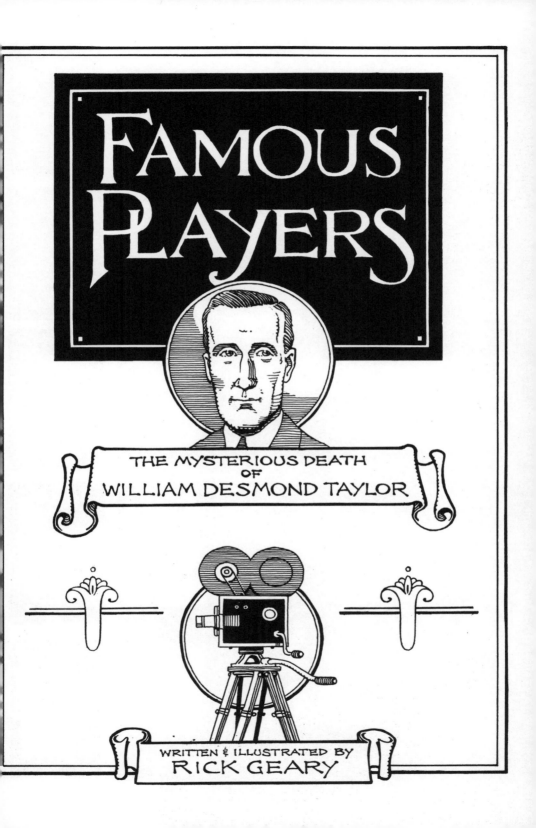

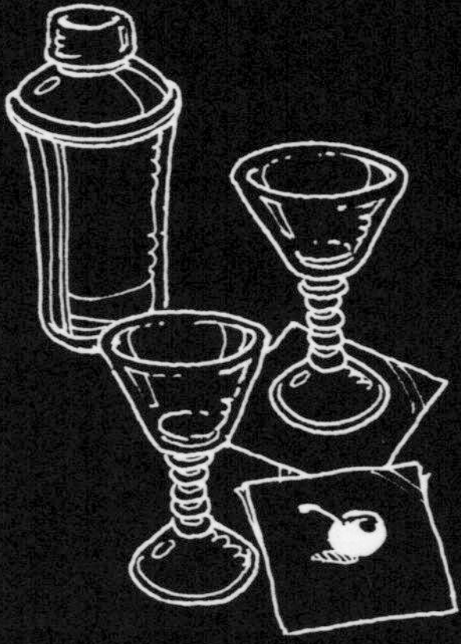

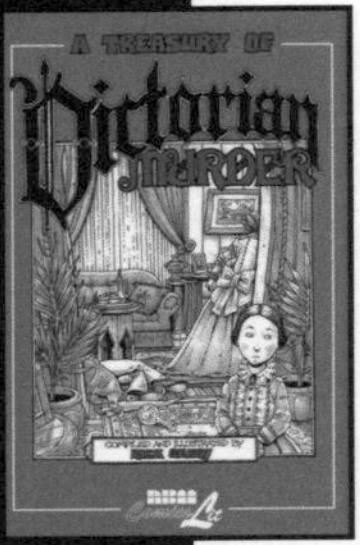
A TREASURY OF
Victorian
MURDER

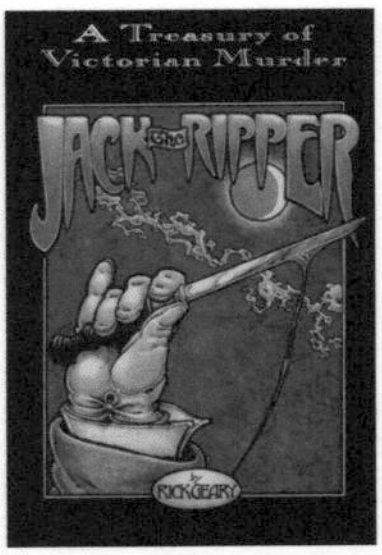
A Treasury of
Victorian Murder
JACK the RIPPER
RICK GEARY

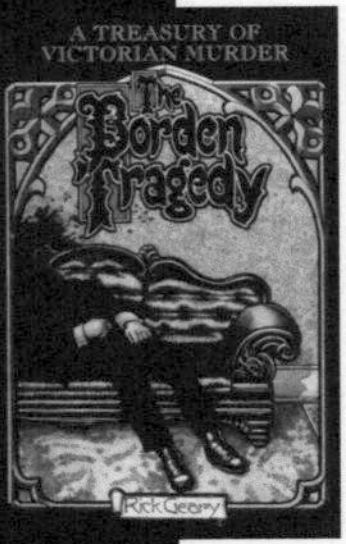
A TREASURY OF
VICTORIAN MURDER
The Borden Tragedy
RICK GEARY

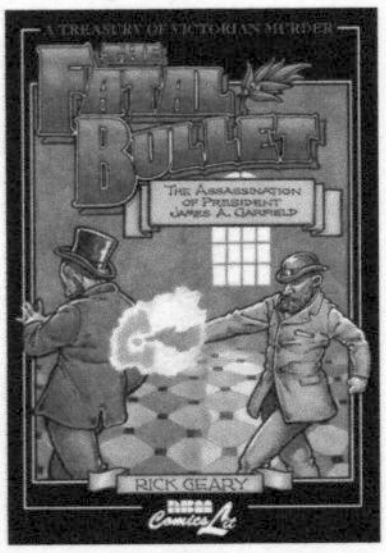
A TREASURY OF VICTORIAN MURDER
FATAL BULLET
THE ASSASSINATION OF PRESIDENT JAMES A. GARFIELD
RICK GEARY

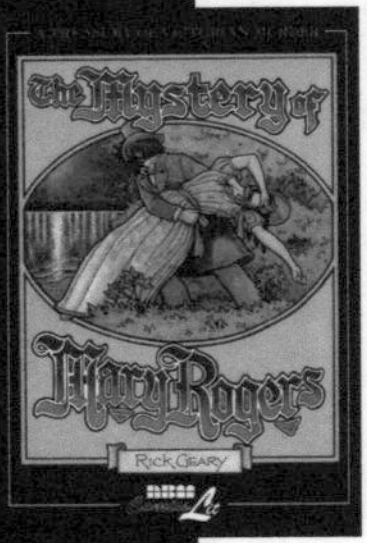
The Mystery of
Mary Rogers
RICK GEARY

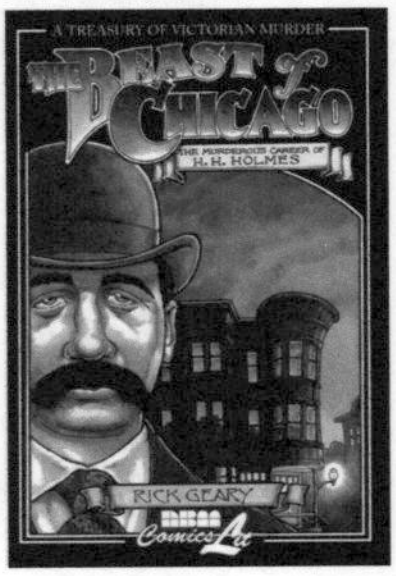
A TREASURY OF VICTORIAN MURDER
The BEAST of CHICAGO
H.H. HOLMES
RICK GEARY

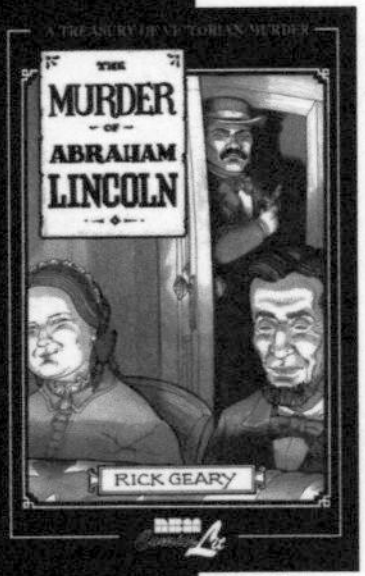
THE
MURDER
OF
ABRAHAM
LINCOLN
RICK GEARY

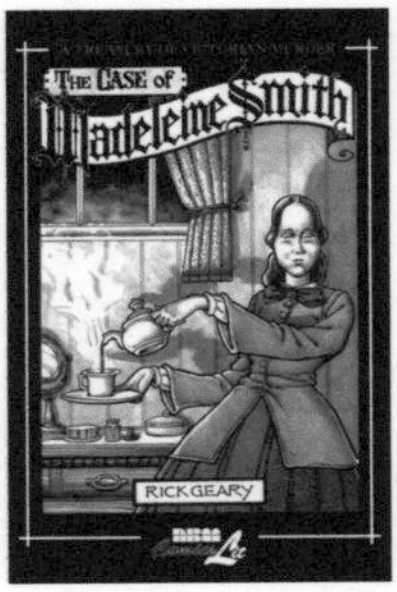
The CASE of
Madeleine Smith
RICK GEARY

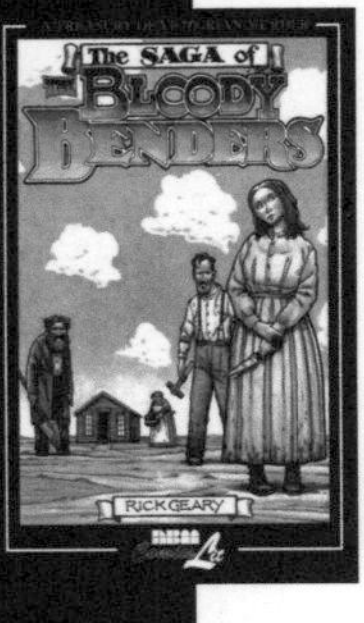
The SAGA of
the BLOODY
BENDERS
RICK GEARY

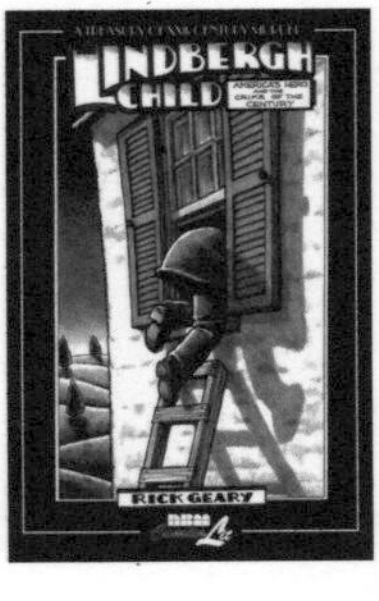
LINDBERGH
CHILD
RICK GEARY

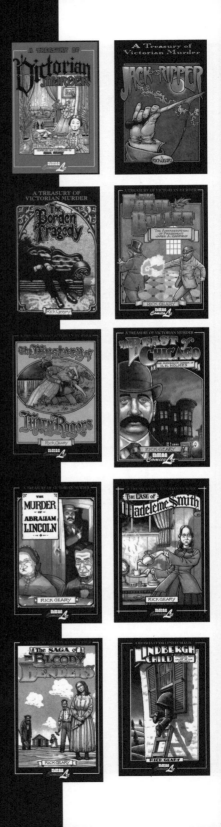

FAMOUS PLAYERS

BIBLIOGRAPHY

Anger, Kenneth, *Hollywood Babylon*. (San Francisco, Straight Arrow Books, 1975)

Gardner, Erle Stanley, "William Desmond Taylor," reprinted in *Los Angeles Murders*. (New York, Duell, Sloan and Pearce, 1947)

Higham, Charles, *Murder in Hollywood, Solving a Silent Screen Mystery*. (Madison WI, University of Wisconsin Press, 2004)

Lamparski, Richard, *Lamparski's Hidden Hollywood*. (New York, Fireside Books, 1981)

Kirkpatrick, Sidney D., *A Cast of Killers*. (New York, Penguin Books, 1986)

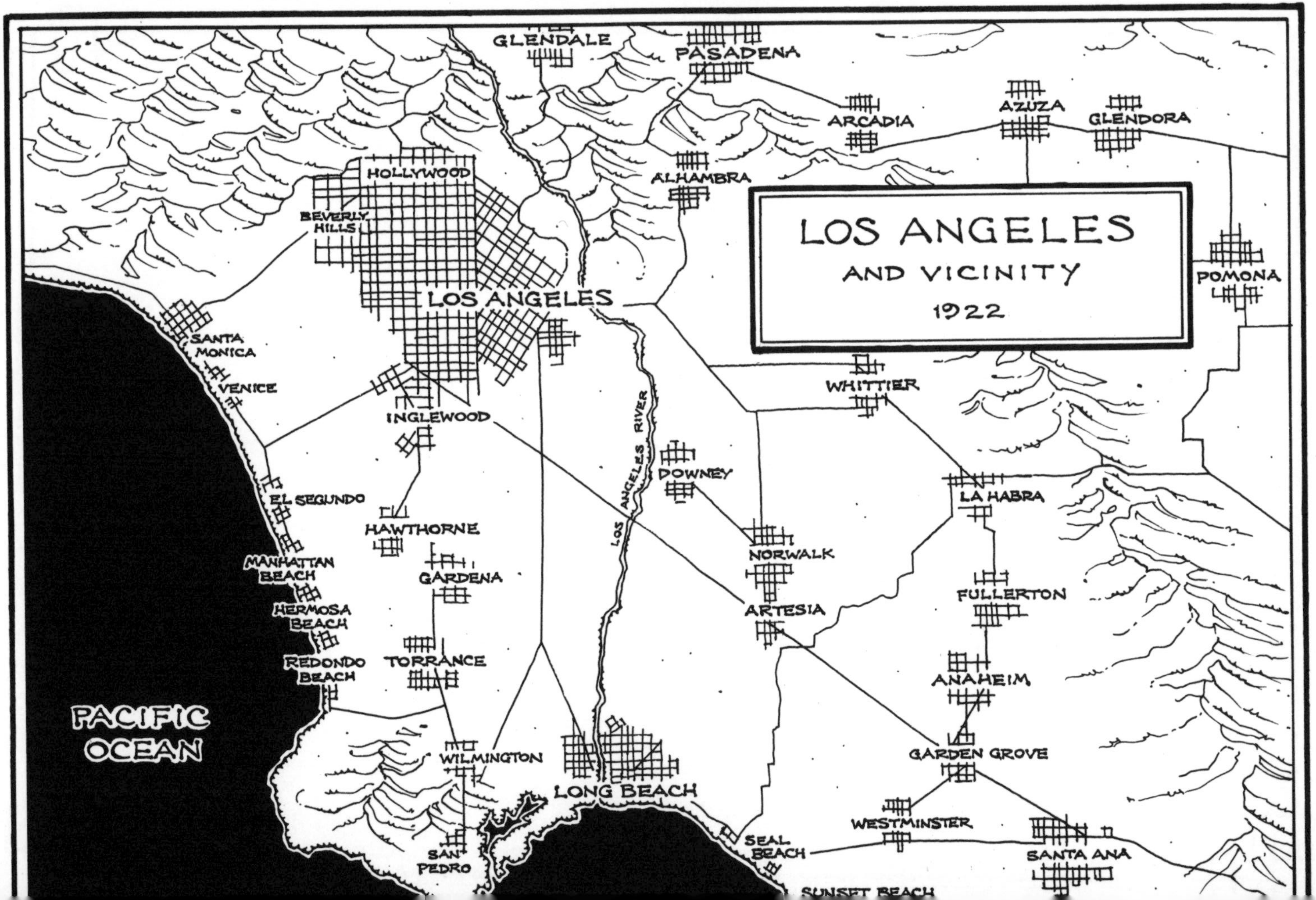
LOS ANGELES
AND VICINITY
1922
GLENDALE
PASADENA
ARCADIA
AZUZA
GLENDORA
ALHAMBRA
POMONA
HOLLYWOOD
BEVERLY HILLS
LOS ANGELES
SANTA MONICA
VENICE
INGLEWOOD
WHITTIER
LOS ANGELES RIVER
DOWNEY
EL SEGUNDO
HAWTHORNE
LA HABRA
NORWALK
MANHATTAN BEACH
GARDENA
FULLERTON
HERMOSA BEACH
ARTESIA
REDONDO BEACH
TORRANCE
ANAHEIM
PACIFIC OCEAN
WILMINGTON
GARDEN GROVE
LONG BEACH
WESTMINSTER
SEAL BEACH
SANTA ANA
SAN PEDRO
SUNSET BEACH

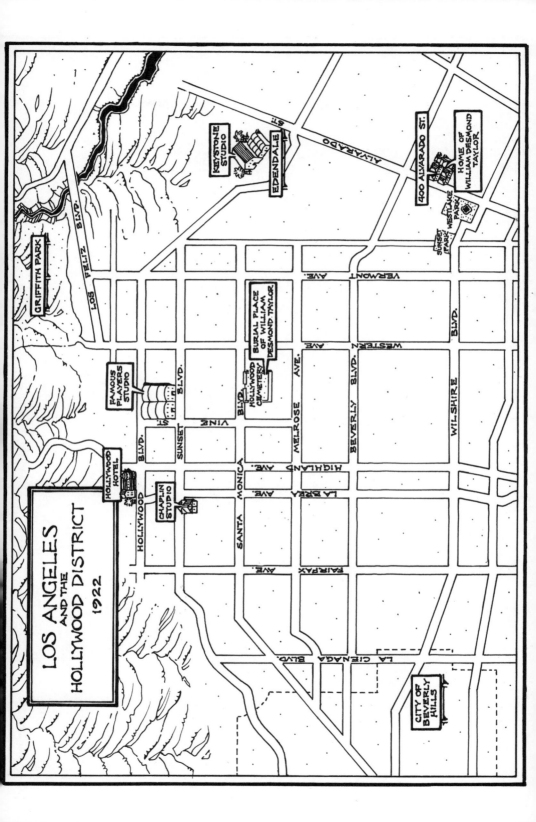

LOS ANGELES
AND THE
HOLLYWOOD DISTRICT
1922

GRIFFITH PARK

LOS FELIZ BLVD.

KEYSTONE STUDIO

EDENDALE ST.

ALVARADO

400 ALVARADO ST.

HOME OF WILLIAM DESMOND TAYLOR

SUNSET PARK

WESTLAKE PARK

VERMONT AVE.

WESTERN BLVD.

WILSHIRE BLVD.

BURIAL PLACE OF WILLIAM DESMOND TAYLOR

HOLLYWOOD CEMETERY

BLVD.

MELROSE AVE.

BEVERLY BLVD.

FAMOUS PLAYERS STUDIO

BLVD.

VINE ST.

SUNSET BLVD.

SANTA MONICA

HIGHLAND AVE.

LA BREA AVE.

HOLLYWOOD HOTEL

HOLLYWOOD BLVD.

CHAPLIN STUDIO

FAIRFAX AVE.

LA CIENAGA BLVD.

CITY OF BEVERLY HILLS

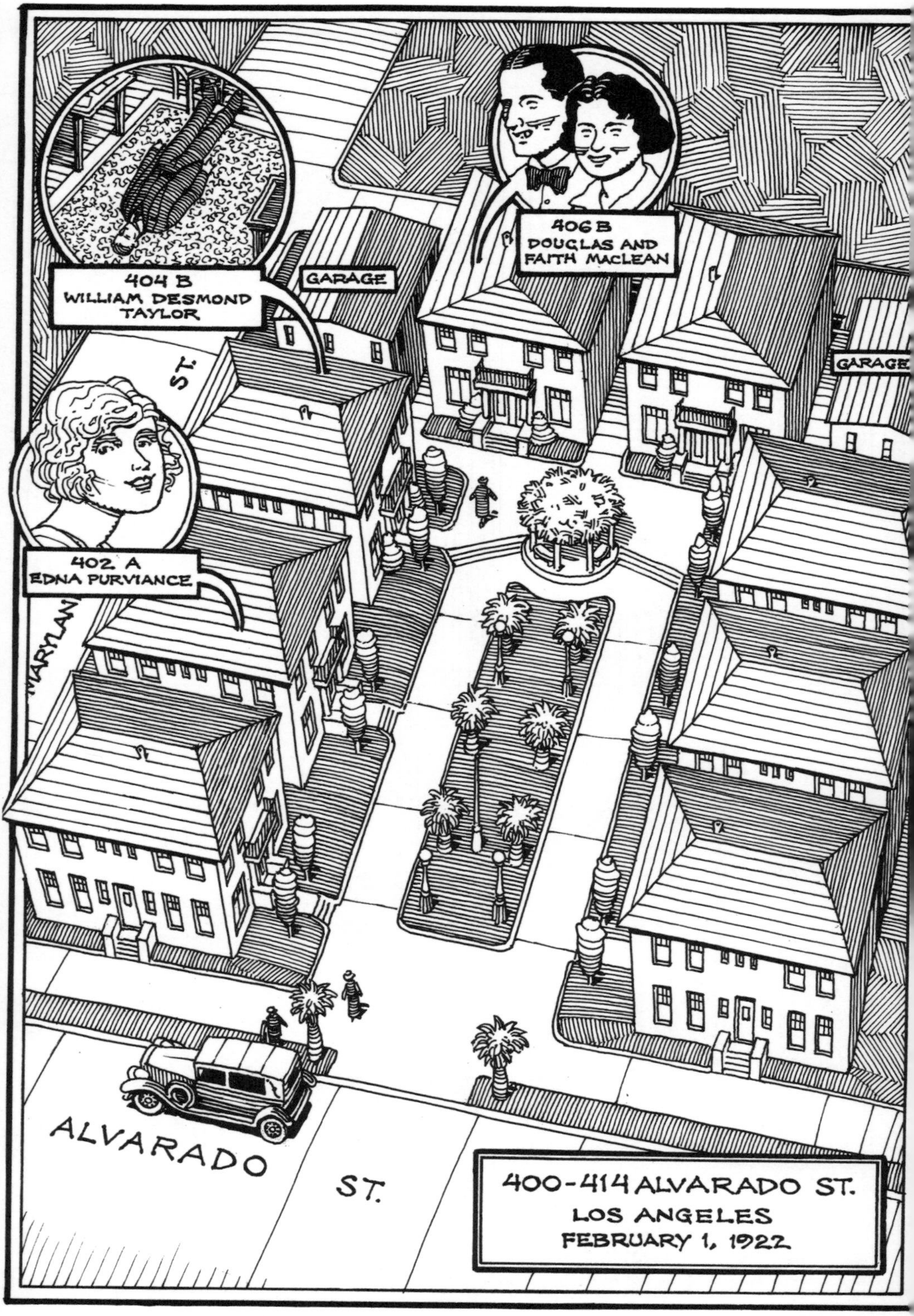
404 B
WILLIAM DESMOND TAYLOR
406 B
DOUGLAS AND FAITH MACLEAN
GARAGE
GARAGE
ST.
MARYLAN
402 A
EDNA PURVIANCE
ALVARADO
ST.
400-414 ALVARADO ST.
LOS ANGELES
FEBRUARY 1, 1922

PART I

THIS IS HOLLYWOOD

STARS OF THE PHOTOPLAY

WILLIAM S. HART

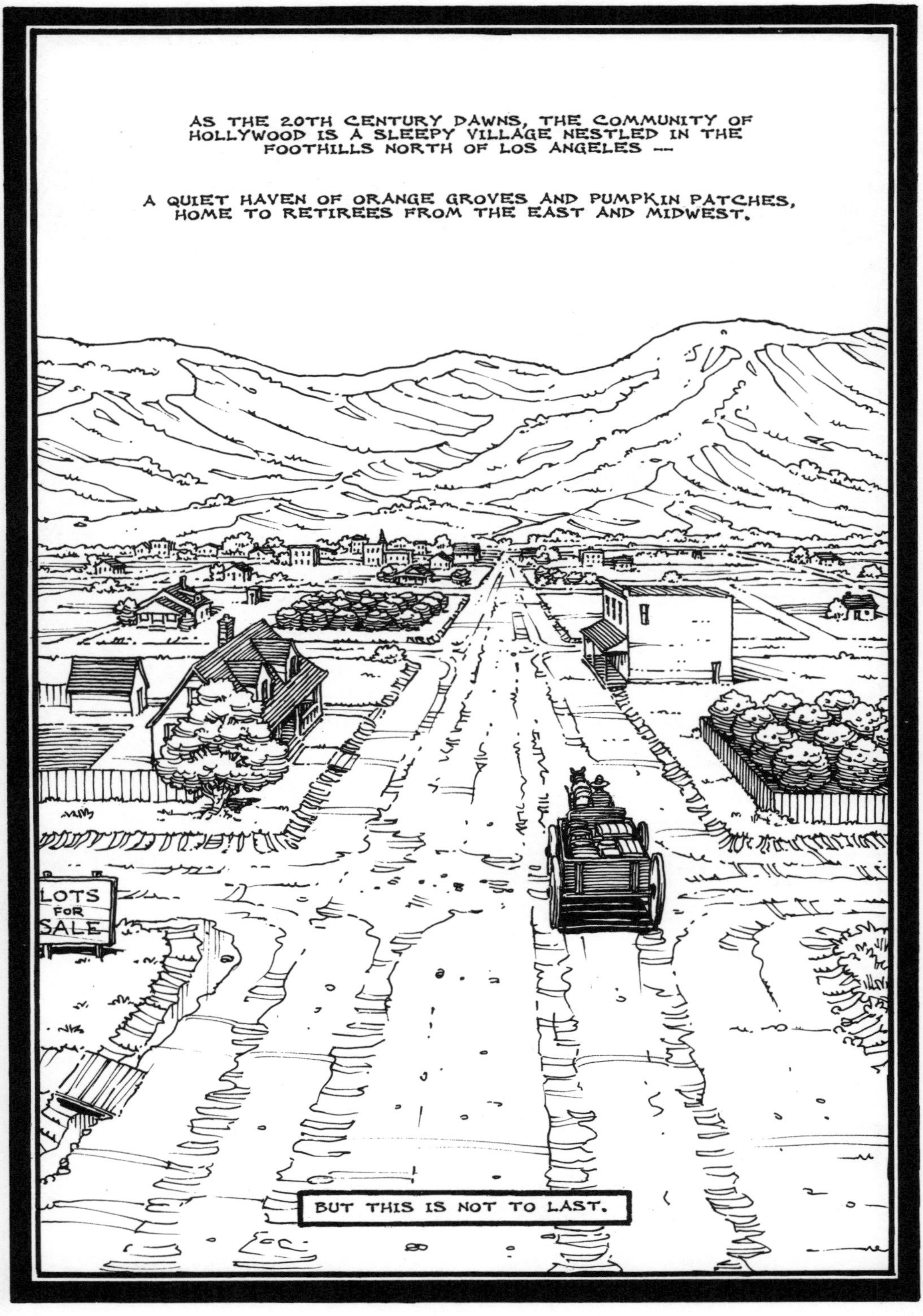
AS THE 20TH CENTURY DAWNS, THE COMMUNITY OF HOLLYWOOD IS A SLEEPY VILLAGE NESTLED IN THE FOOTHILLS NORTH OF LOS ANGELES --
A QUIET HAVEN OF ORANGE GROVES AND PUMPKIN PATCHES, HOME TO RETIREES FROM THE EAST AND MIDWEST.
LOTS FOR SALE
BUT THIS IS NOT TO LAST.

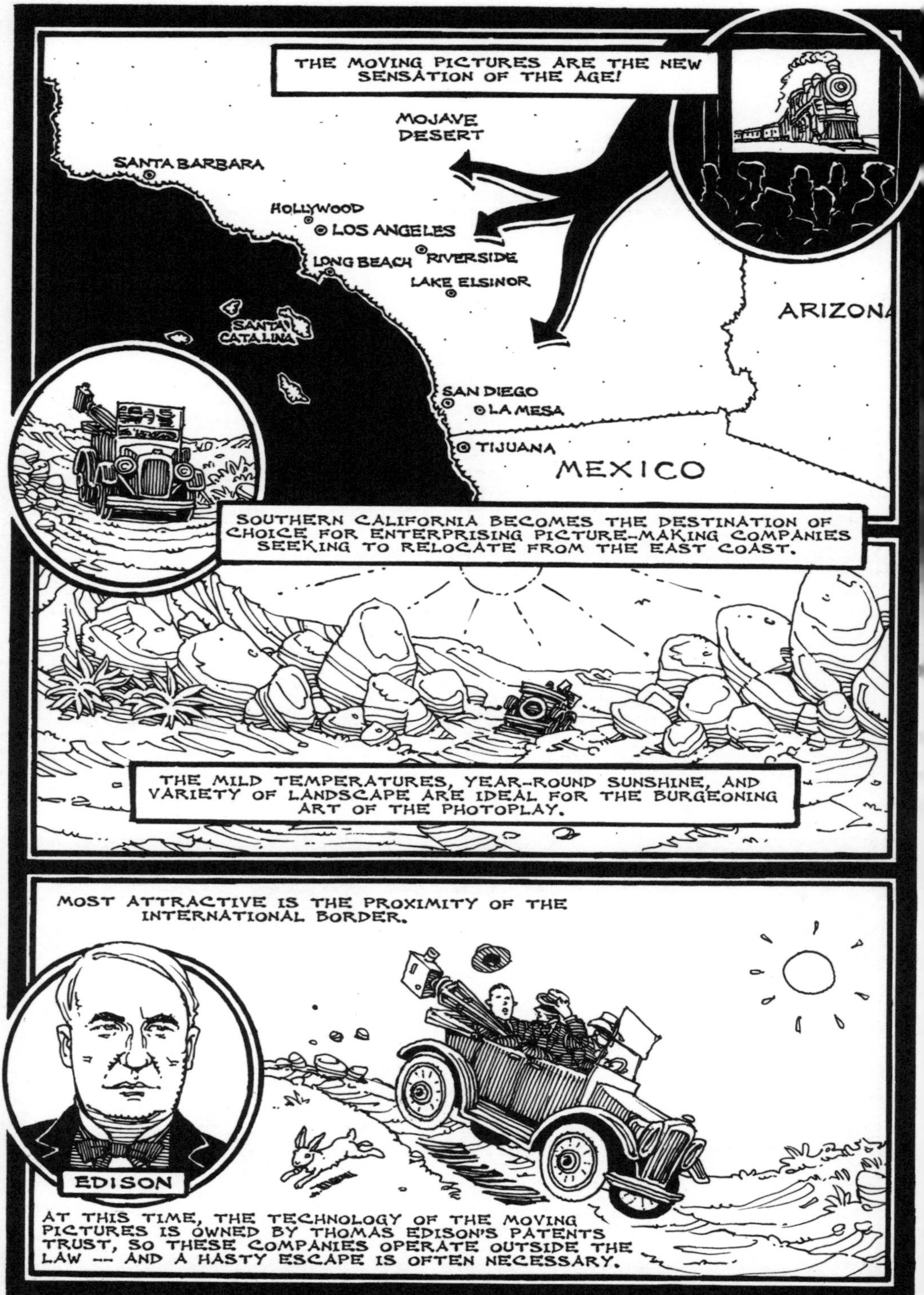
THE MOVING PICTURES ARE THE NEW SENSATION OF THE AGE!
MOJAVE DESERT
SANTA BARBARA
HOLLYWOOD
LOS ANGELES
LONG BEACH
RIVERSIDE
LAKE ELSINOR
SANTA CATALINA
ARIZONA
SAN DIEGO
LA MESA
TIJUANA
MEXICO
SOUTHERN CALIFORNIA BECOMES THE DESTINATION OF CHOICE FOR ENTERPRISING PICTURE-MAKING COMPANIES SEEKING TO RELOCATE FROM THE EAST COAST.
THE MILD TEMPERATURES, YEAR-ROUND SUNSHINE, AND VARIETY OF LANDSCAPE ARE IDEAL FOR THE BURGEONING ART OF THE PHOTOPLAY.
MOST ATTRACTIVE IS THE PROXIMITY OF THE INTERNATIONAL BORDER.
EDISON
AT THIS TIME, THE TECHNOLOGY OF THE MOVING PICTURES IS OWNED BY THOMAS EDISON'S PATENTS TRUST, SO THESE COMPANIES OPERATE OUTSIDE THE LAW -- AND A HASTY ESCAPE IS OFTEN NECESSARY.

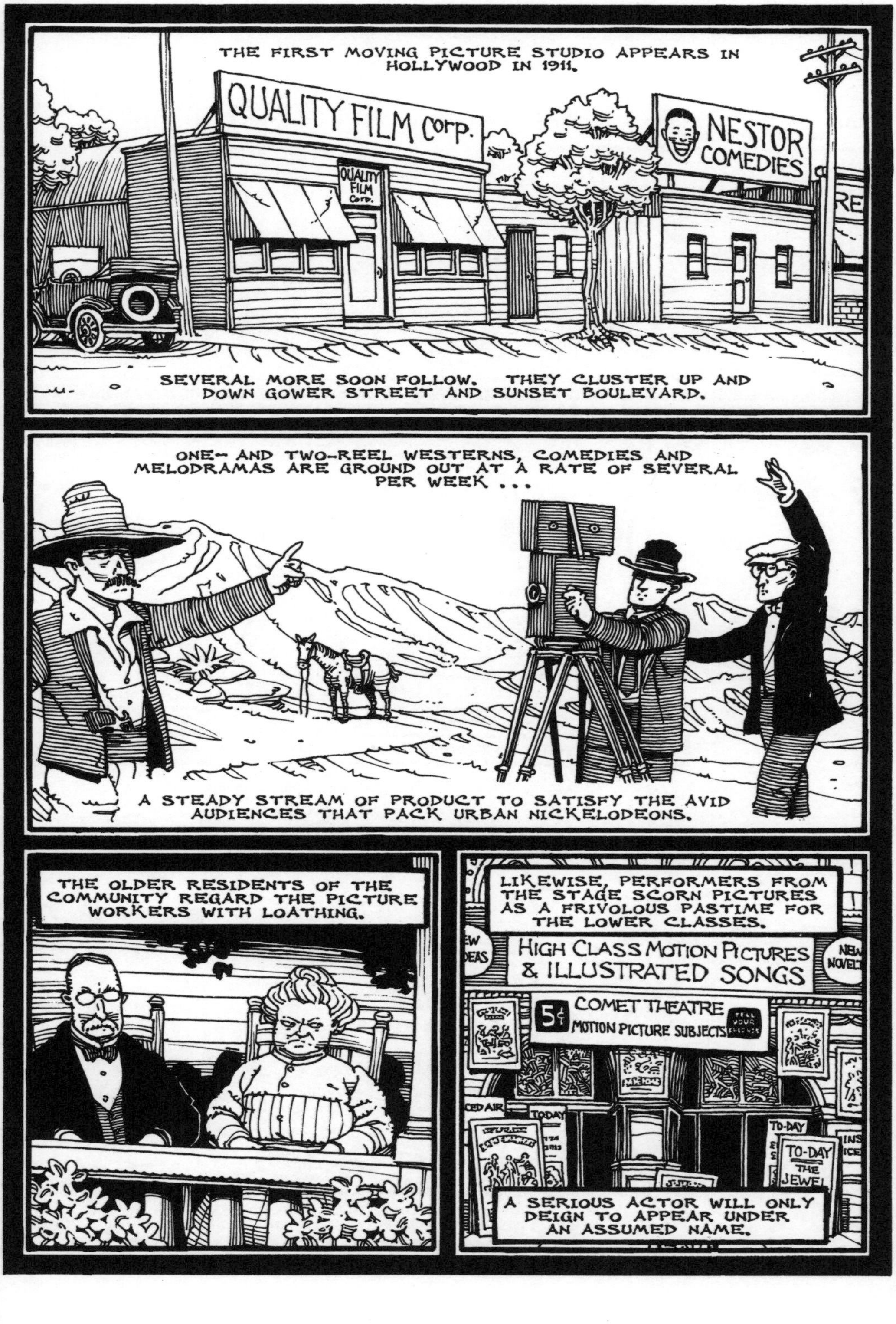

THE FIRST MOVING PICTURE STUDIO APPEARS IN HOLLYWOOD IN 1911.
QUALITY FILM Corp.
NESTOR COMEDIES
SEVERAL MORE SOON FOLLOW. THEY CLUSTER UP AND DOWN GOWER STREET AND SUNSET BOULEVARD.
ONE- AND TWO-REEL WESTERNS, COMEDIES AND MELODRAMAS ARE GROUND OUT AT A RATE OF SEVERAL PER WEEK ...
A STEADY STREAM OF PRODUCT TO SATISFY THE AVID AUDIENCES THAT PACK URBAN NICKELODEONS.
THE OLDER RESIDENTS OF THE COMMUNITY REGARD THE PICTURE WORKERS WITH LOATHING.
LIKEWISE, PERFORMERS FROM THE STAGE SCORN PICTURES AS A FRIVOLOUS PASTIME FOR THE LOWER CLASSES.
HIGH CLASS MOTION PICTURES & ILLUSTRATED SONGS
5¢ COMET THEATRE MOTION PICTURE SUBJECTS
TODAY
TO-DAY
A SERIOUS ACTOR WILL ONLY DEIGN TO APPEAR UNDER AN ASSUMED NAME.

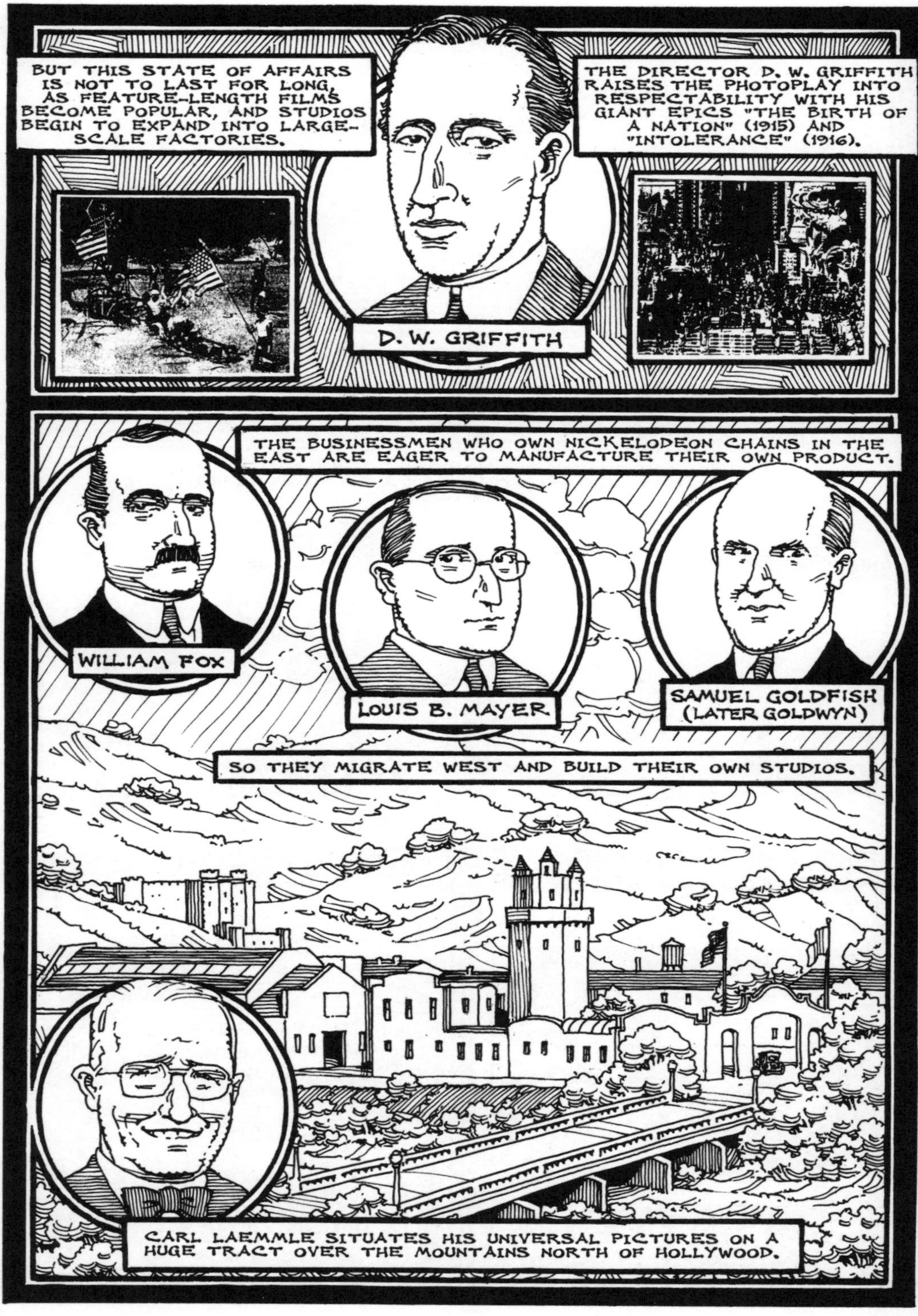
BUT THIS STATE OF AFFAIRS IS NOT TO LAST FOR LONG, AS FEATURE-LENGTH FILMS BECOME POPULAR, AND STUDIOS BEGIN TO EXPAND INTO LARGE-SCALE FACTORIES.
THE DIRECTOR D. W. GRIFFITH RAISES THE PHOTOPLAY INTO RESPECTABILITY WITH HIS GIANT EPICS "THE BIRTH OF A NATION" (1915) AND "INTOLERANCE" (1916).
D. W. GRIFFITH
THE BUSINESSMEN WHO OWN NICKELODEON CHAINS IN THE EAST ARE EAGER TO MANUFACTURE THEIR OWN PRODUCT.
WILLIAM FOX
LOUIS B. MAYER
SAMUEL GOLDFISH (LATER GOLDWYN)
SO THEY MIGRATE WEST AND BUILD THEIR OWN STUDIOS.
CARL LAEMMLE SITUATES HIS UNIVERSAL PICTURES ON A HUGE TRACT OVER THE MOUNTAINS NORTH OF HOLLYWOOD.

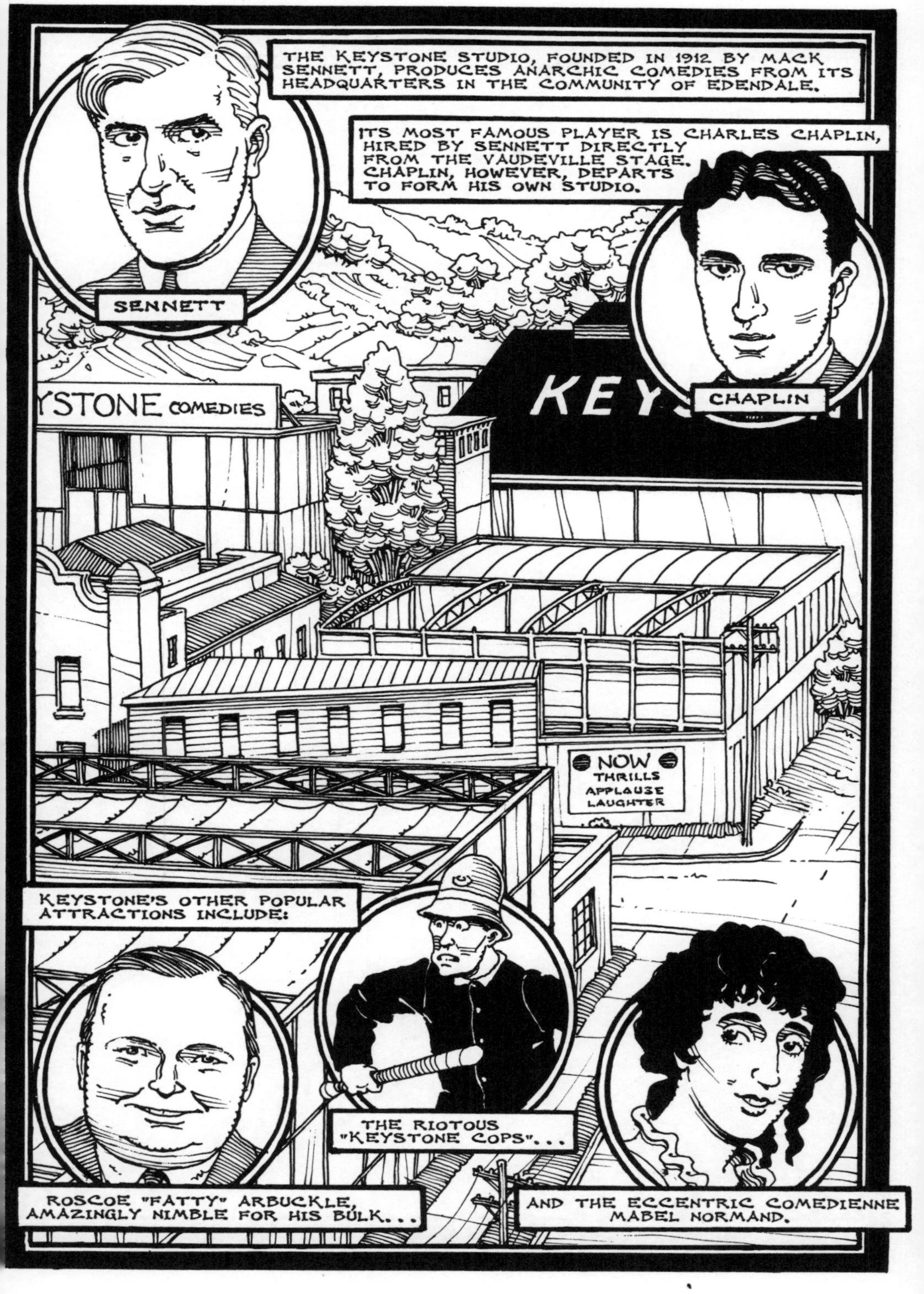
THE KEYSTONE STUDIO, FOUNDED IN 1912 BY MACK SENNETT, PRODUCES ANARCHIC COMEDIES FROM ITS HEADQUARTERS IN THE COMMUNITY OF EDENDALE.
ITS MOST FAMOUS PLAYER IS CHARLES CHAPLIN, HIRED BY SENNETT DIRECTLY FROM THE VAUDEVILLE STAGE. CHAPLIN, HOWEVER, DEPARTS TO FORM HIS OWN STUDIO.
SENNETT
CHAPLIN
YSTONE COMEDIES
KEY
NOW
THRILLS
APPLAUSE
LAUGHTER
KEYSTONE'S OTHER POPULAR ATTRACTIONS INCLUDE:
ROSCOE "FATTY" ARBUCKLE, AMAZINGLY NIMBLE FOR HIS BULK...
THE RIOTOUS "KEYSTONE COPS"...
AND THE ECCENTRIC COMEDIENNE MABEL NORMAND.

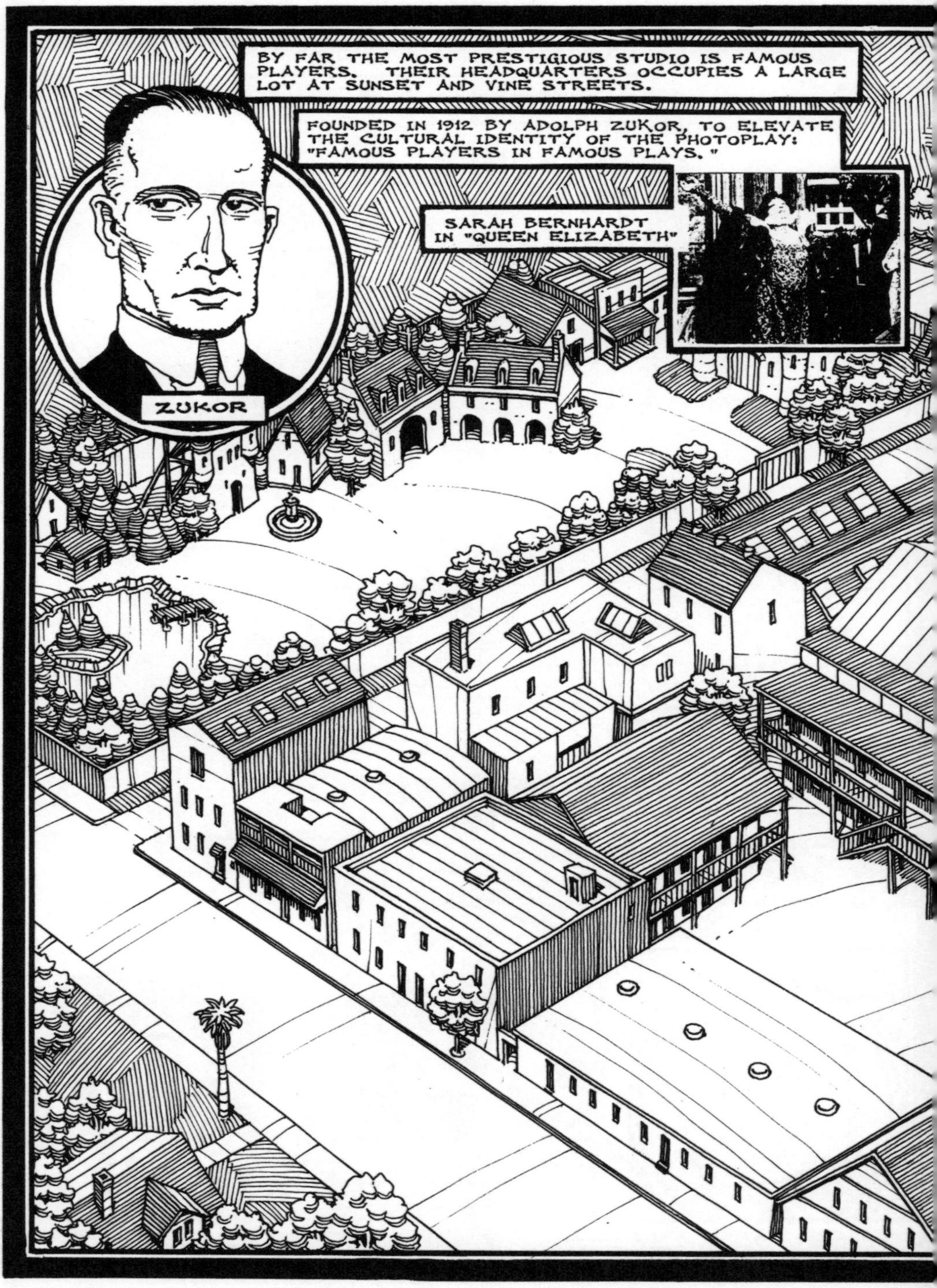
BY FAR THE MOST PRESTIGIOUS STUDIO IS FAMOUS PLAYERS. THEIR HEADQUARTERS OCCUPIES A LARGE LOT AT SUNSET AND VINE STREETS.
FOUNDED IN 1912 BY ADOLPH ZUKOR, TO ELEVATE THE CULTURAL IDENTITY OF THE PHOTOPLAY: "FAMOUS PLAYERS IN FAMOUS PLAYS."
SARAH BERNHARDT IN "QUEEN ELIZABETH"
ZUKOR

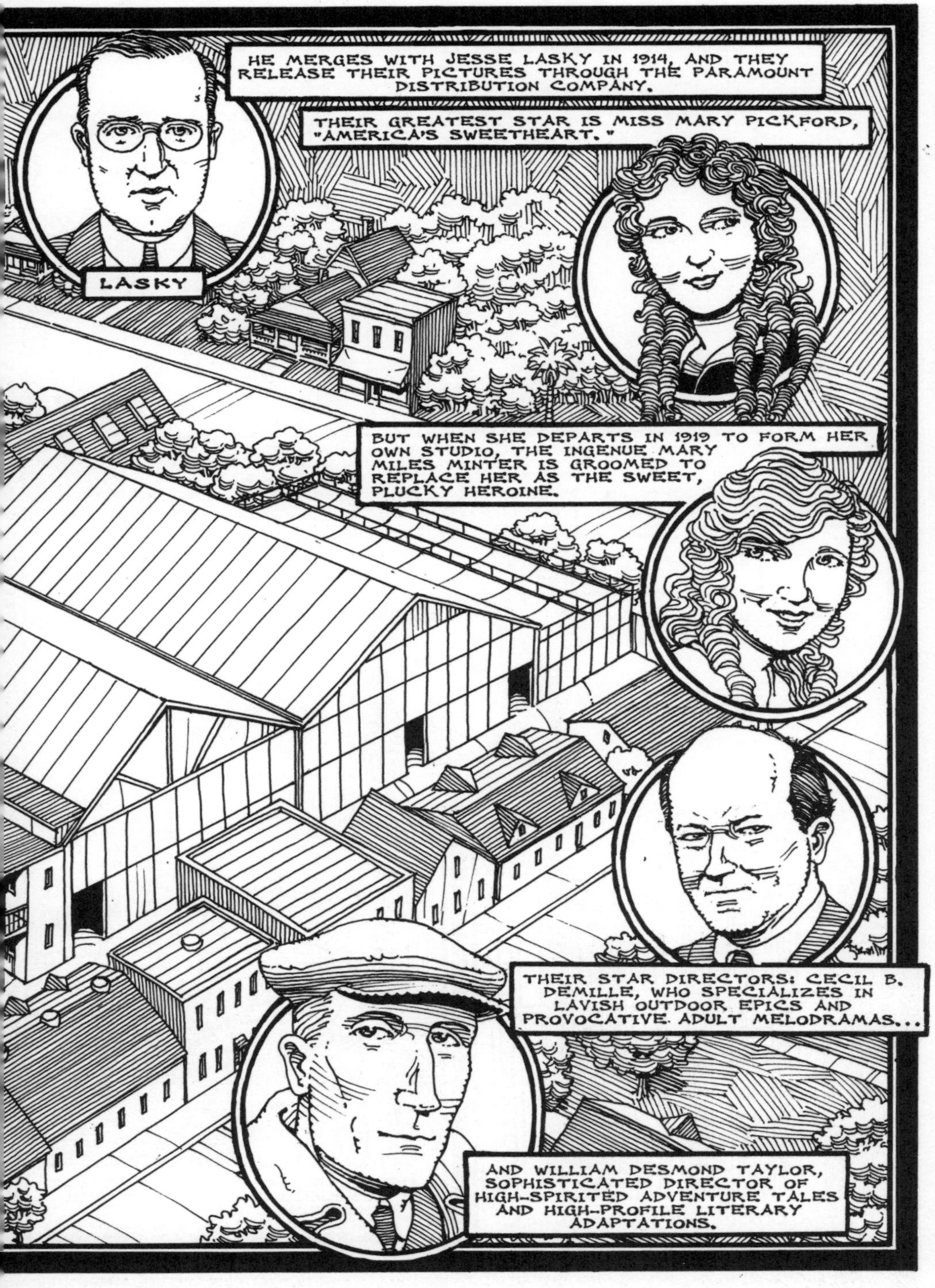
HE MERGES WITH JESSE LASKY IN 1914, AND THEY RELEASE THEIR PICTURES THROUGH THE PARAMOUNT DISTRIBUTION COMPANY.
LASKY
THEIR GREATEST STAR IS MISS MARY PICKFORD, "AMERICA'S SWEETHEART."
BUT WHEN SHE DEPARTS IN 1919 TO FORM HER OWN STUDIO, THE INGENUE MARY MILES MINTER IS GROOMED TO REPLACE HER AS THE SWEET, PLUCKY HEROINE.
THEIR STAR DIRECTORS: CECIL B. DEMILLE, WHO SPECIALIZES IN LAVISH OUTDOOR EPICS AND PROVOCATIVE ADULT MELODRAMAS...
AND WILLIAM DESMOND TAYLOR, SOPHISTICATED DIRECTOR OF HIGH-SPIRITED ADVENTURE TALES AND HIGH-PROFILE LITERARY ADAPTATIONS.

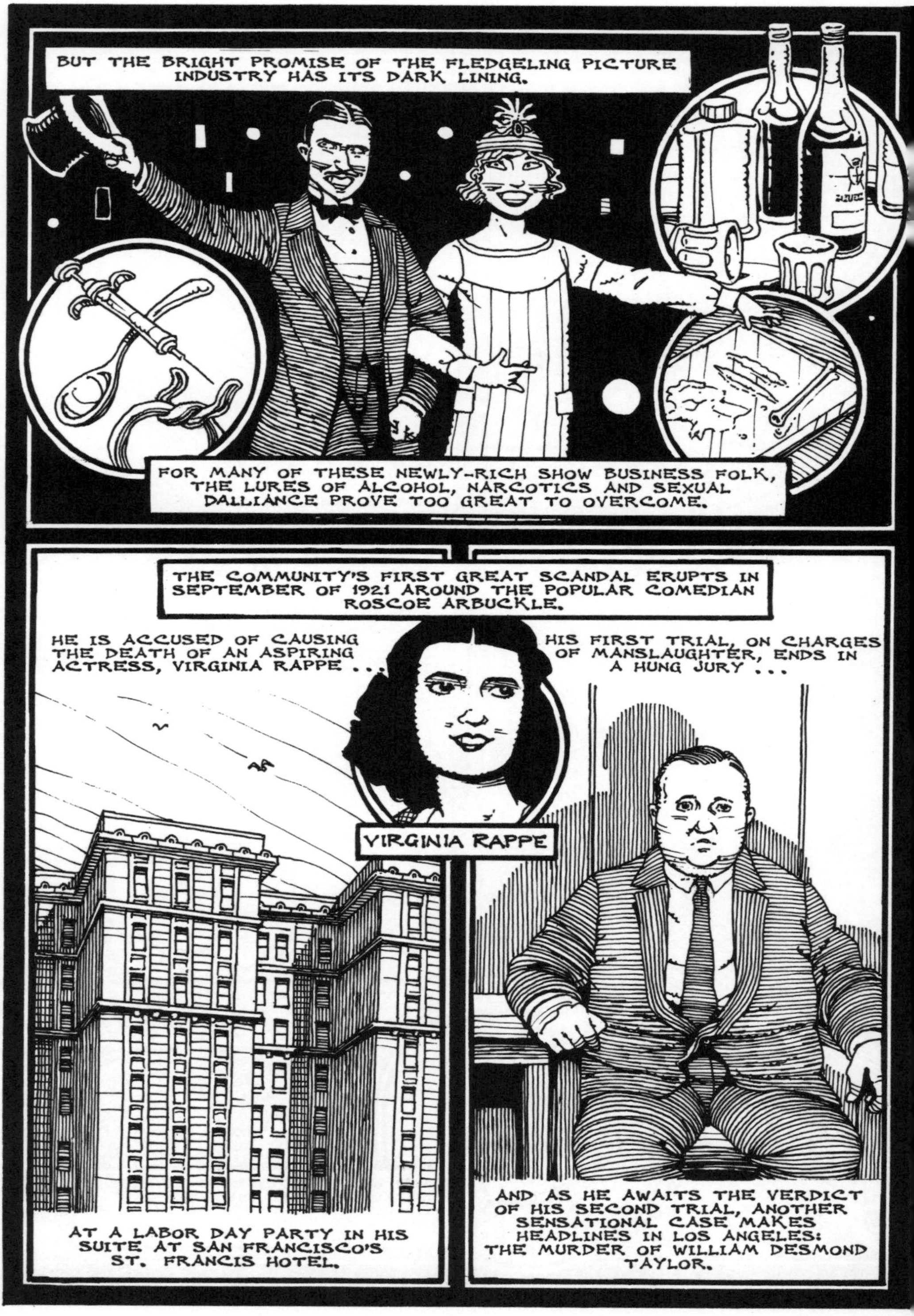

BUT THE BRIGHT PROMISE OF THE FLEDGELING PICTURE INDUSTRY HAS ITS DARK LINING.
FOR MANY OF THESE NEWLY-RICH SHOW BUSINESS FOLK, THE LURES OF ALCOHOL, NARCOTICS AND SEXUAL DALLIANCE PROVE TOO GREAT TO OVERCOME.
THE COMMUNITY'S FIRST GREAT SCANDAL ERUPTS IN SEPTEMBER OF 1921 AROUND THE POPULAR COMEDIAN ROSCOE ARBUCKLE.
HE IS ACCUSED OF CAUSING THE DEATH OF AN ASPIRING ACTRESS, VIRGINIA RAPPE ...
VIRGINIA RAPPE
AT A LABOR DAY PARTY IN HIS SUITE AT SAN FRANCISCO'S ST. FRANCIS HOTEL.
HIS FIRST TRIAL, ON CHARGES OF MANSLAUGHTER, ENDS IN A HUNG JURY ...
AND AS HE AWAITS THE VERDICT OF HIS SECOND TRIAL, ANOTHER SENSATIONAL CASE MAKES HEADLINES IN LOS ANGELES: THE MURDER OF WILLIAM DESMOND TAYLOR.

PART II

THE DISCOVERY OF
THE BODY

STARS OF THE PHOTOPLAY

GLORIA SWANSON

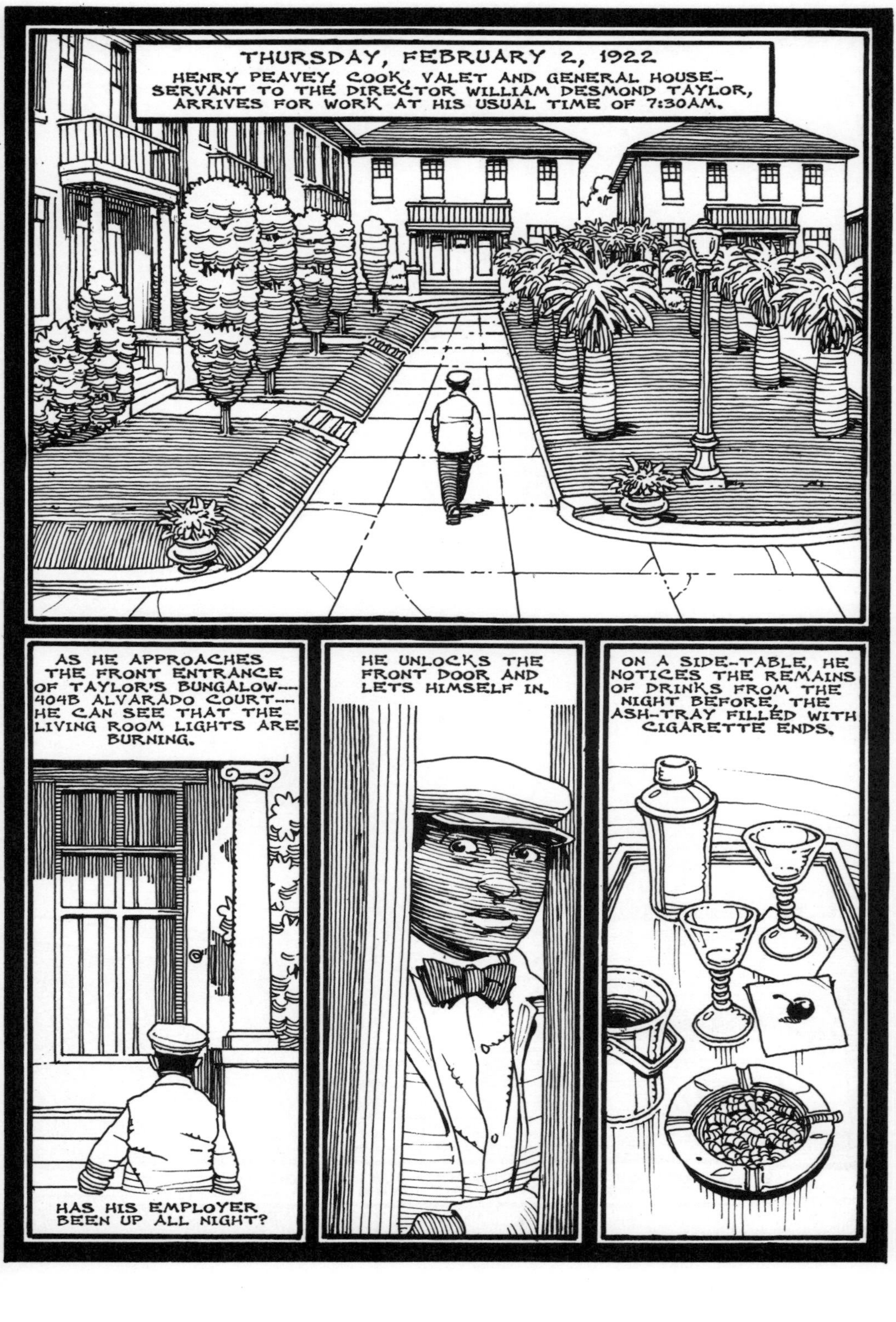
THURSDAY, FEBRUARY 2, 1922
HENRY PEAVEY, COOK, VALET AND GENERAL HOUSE-SERVANT TO THE DIRECTOR WILLIAM DESMOND TAYLOR, ARRIVES FOR WORK AT HIS USUAL TIME OF 7:30AM.
AS HE APPROACHES THE FRONT ENTRANCE OF TAYLOR'S BUNGALOW--- 404B ALVARADO COURT--- HE CAN SEE THAT THE LIVING ROOM LIGHTS ARE BURNING.
HAS HIS EMPLOYER BEEN UP ALL NIGHT?
HE UNLOCKS THE FRONT DOOR AND LETS HIMSELF IN.
ON A SIDE-TABLE, HE NOTICES THE REMAINS OF DRINKS FROM THE NIGHT BEFORE, THE ASH-TRAY FILLED WITH CIGARETTE ENDS.

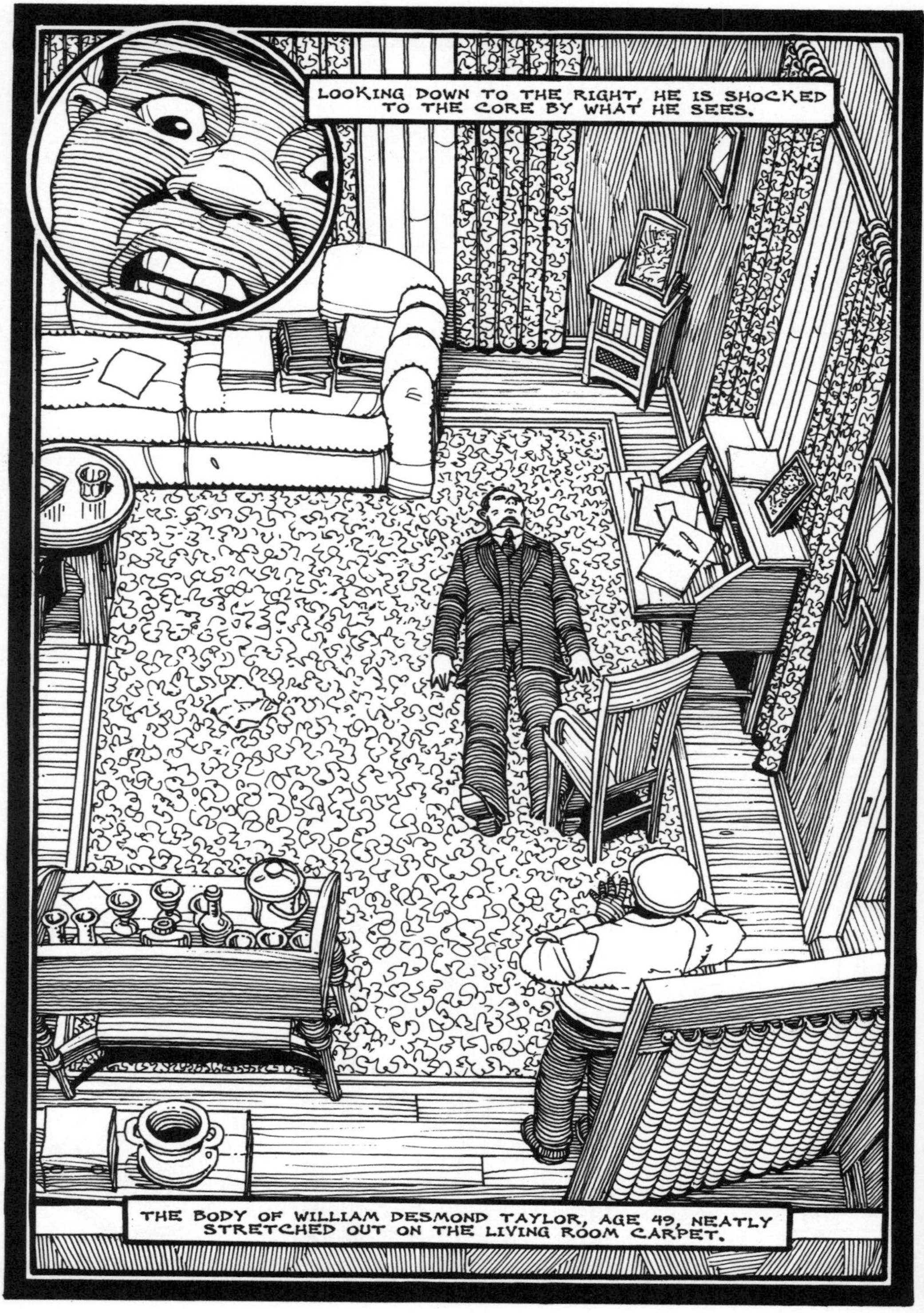
LOOKING DOWN TO THE RIGHT, HE IS SHOCKED TO THE CORE BY WHAT HE SEES.
THE BODY OF WILLIAM DESMOND TAYLOR, AGE 49, NEATLY STRETCHED OUT ON THE LIVING ROOM CARPET.

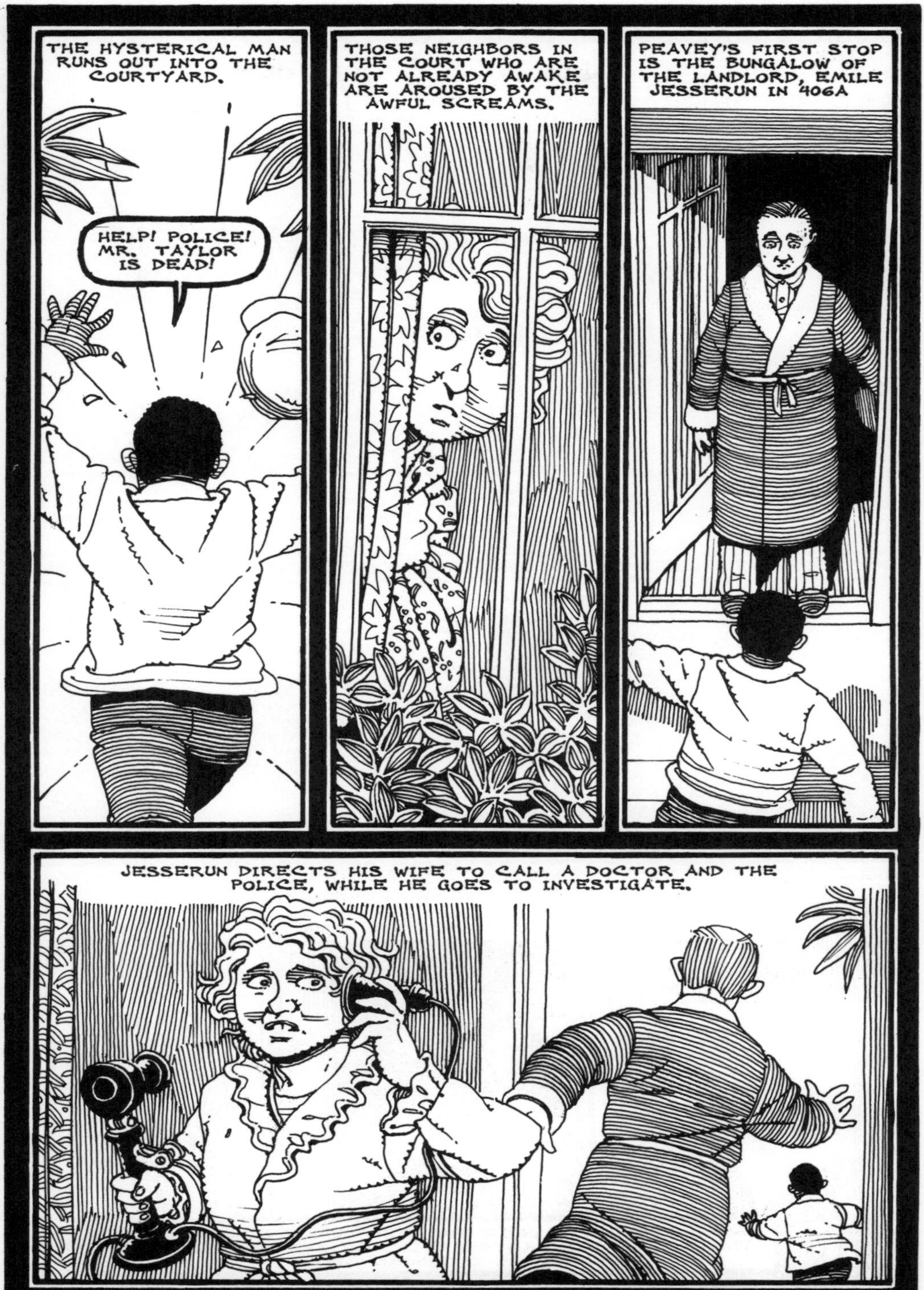
THE HYSTERICAL MAN RUNS OUT INTO THE COURTYARD.
HELP! POLICE! MR. TAYLOR IS DEAD!
THOSE NEIGHBORS IN THE COURT WHO ARE NOT ALREADY AWAKE ARE AROUSED BY THE AWFUL SCREAMS.
PEAVEY'S FIRST STOP IS THE BUNGALOW OF THE LANDLORD, EMILE JESSERUN IN 406A
JESSERUN DIRECTS HIS WIFE TO CALL A DOCTOR AND THE POLICE, WHILE HE GOES TO INVESTIGATE.

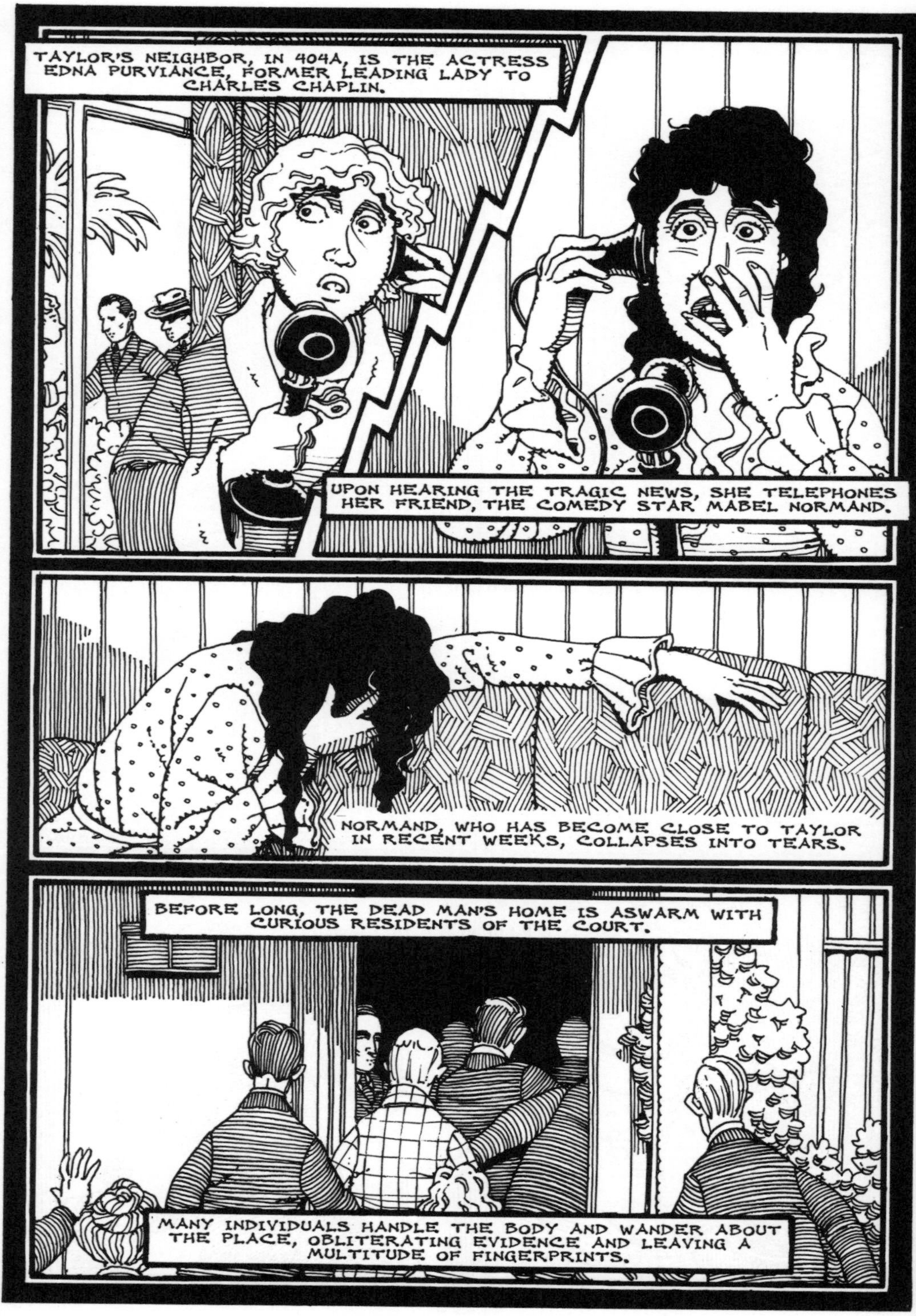
TAYLOR'S NEIGHBOR, IN 404A, IS THE ACTRESS EDNA PURVIANCE, FORMER LEADING LADY TO CHARLES CHAPLIN.
UPON HEARING THE TRAGIC NEWS, SHE TELEPHONES HER FRIEND, THE COMEDY STAR MABEL NORMAND.
NORMAND, WHO HAS BECOME CLOSE TO TAYLOR IN RECENT WEEKS, COLLAPSES INTO TEARS.
BEFORE LONG, THE DEAD MAN'S HOME IS ASWARM WITH CURIOUS RESIDENTS OF THE COURT.
MANY INDIVIDUALS HANDLE THE BODY AND WANDER ABOUT THE PLACE, OBLITERATING EVIDENCE AND LEAVING A MULTITUDE OF FINGERPRINTS.

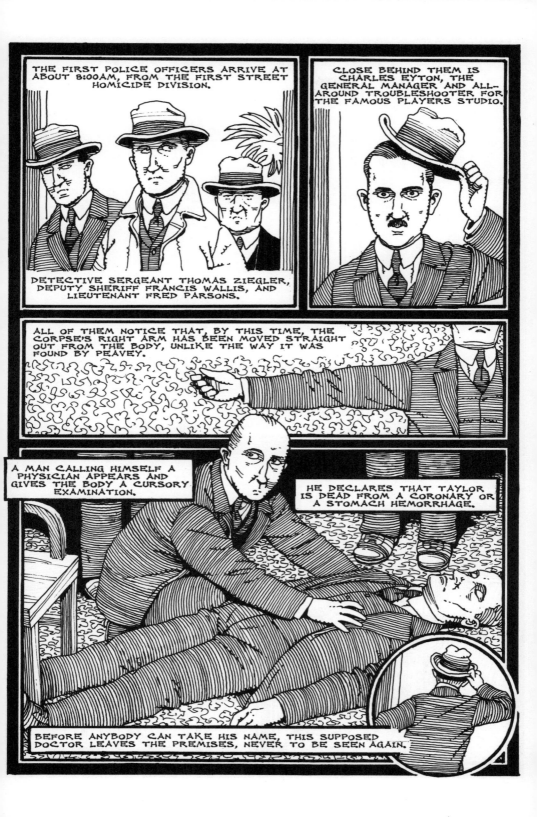

THE FIRST POLICE OFFICERS ARRIVE AT ABOUT 8:00AM, FROM THE FIRST STREET HOMICIDE DIVISION.

CLOSE BEHIND THEM IS CHARLES EYTON, THE GENERAL MANAGER AND ALL-AROUND TROUBLESHOOTER FOR THE FAMOUS PLAYERS STUDIO.

DETECTIVE SERGEANT THOMAS ZIEGLER, DEPUTY SHERIFF FRANCIS WALLIS, AND LIEUTENANT FRED PARSONS.

ALL OF THEM NOTICE THAT, BY THIS TIME, THE CORPSE'S RIGHT ARM HAS BEEN MOVED STRAIGHT OUT FROM THE BODY, UNLIKE THE WAY IT WAS FOUND BY PEAVEY.

A MAN CALLING HIMSELF A PHYSICIAN APPEARS AND GIVES THE BODY A CURSORY EXAMINATION.

HE DECLARES THAT TAYLOR IS DEAD FROM A CORONARY OR A STOMACH HEMORRHAGE.

BEFORE ANYBODY CAN TAKE HIS NAME, THIS SUPPOSED DOCTOR LEAVES THE PREMISES, NEVER TO BE SEEN AGAIN.

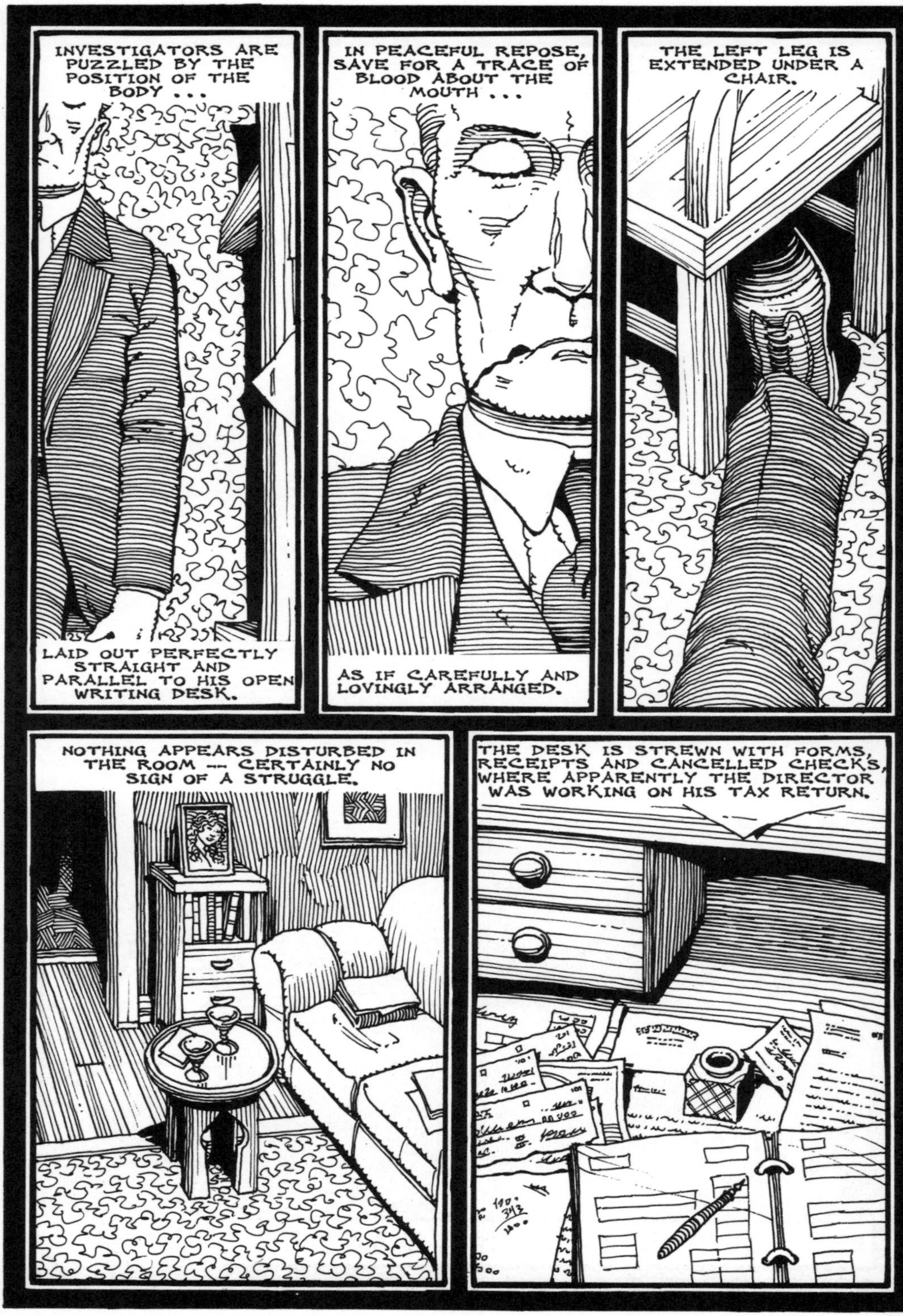
INVESTIGATORS ARE PUZZLED BY THE POSITION OF THE BODY ...
LAID OUT PERFECTLY STRAIGHT AND PARALLEL TO HIS OPEN WRITING DESK.
IN PEACEFUL REPOSE, SAVE FOR A TRACE OF BLOOD ABOUT THE MOUTH ...
AS IF CAREFULLY AND LOVINGLY ARRANGED.
THE LEFT LEG IS EXTENDED UNDER A CHAIR.
NOTHING APPEARS DISTURBED IN THE ROOM -- CERTAINLY NO SIGN OF A STRUGGLE.
THE DESK IS STREWN WITH FORMS, RECEIPTS AND CANCELLED CHECKS, WHERE APPARENTLY THE DIRECTOR WAS WORKING ON HIS TAX RETURN.

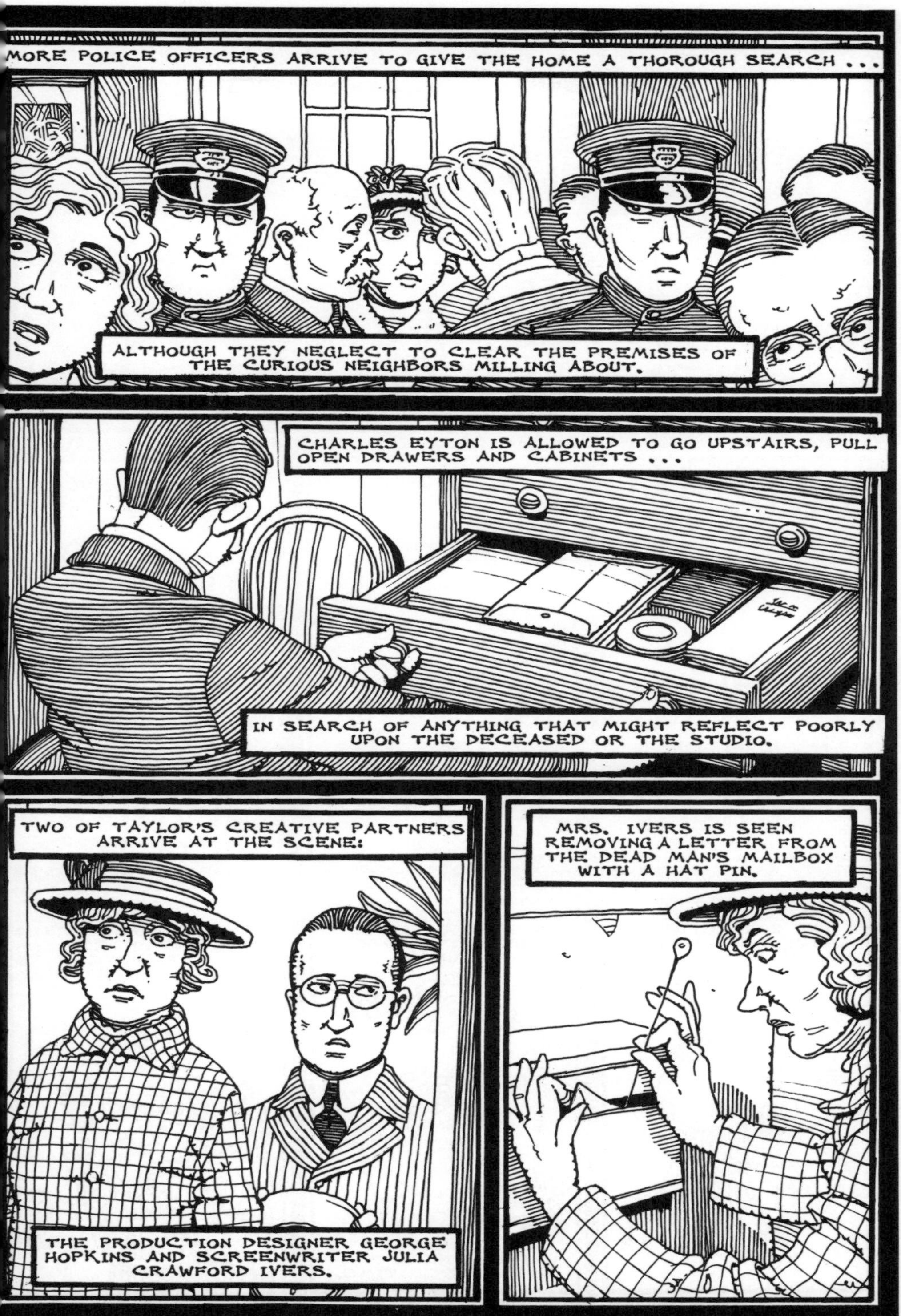
MORE POLICE OFFICERS ARRIVE TO GIVE THE HOME A THOROUGH SEARCH ...
ALTHOUGH THEY NEGLECT TO CLEAR THE PREMISES OF THE CURIOUS NEIGHBORS MILLING ABOUT.
CHARLES EYTON IS ALLOWED TO GO UPSTAIRS, PULL OPEN DRAWERS AND CABINETS ...
IN SEARCH OF ANYTHING THAT MIGHT REFLECT POORLY UPON THE DECEASED OR THE STUDIO.
TWO OF TAYLOR'S CREATIVE PARTNERS ARRIVE AT THE SCENE:
THE PRODUCTION DESIGNER GEORGE HOPKINS AND SCREENWRITER JULIA CRAWFORD IVERS.
MRS. IVERS IS SEEN REMOVING A LETTER FROM THE DEAD MAN'S MAILBOX WITH A HAT PIN.

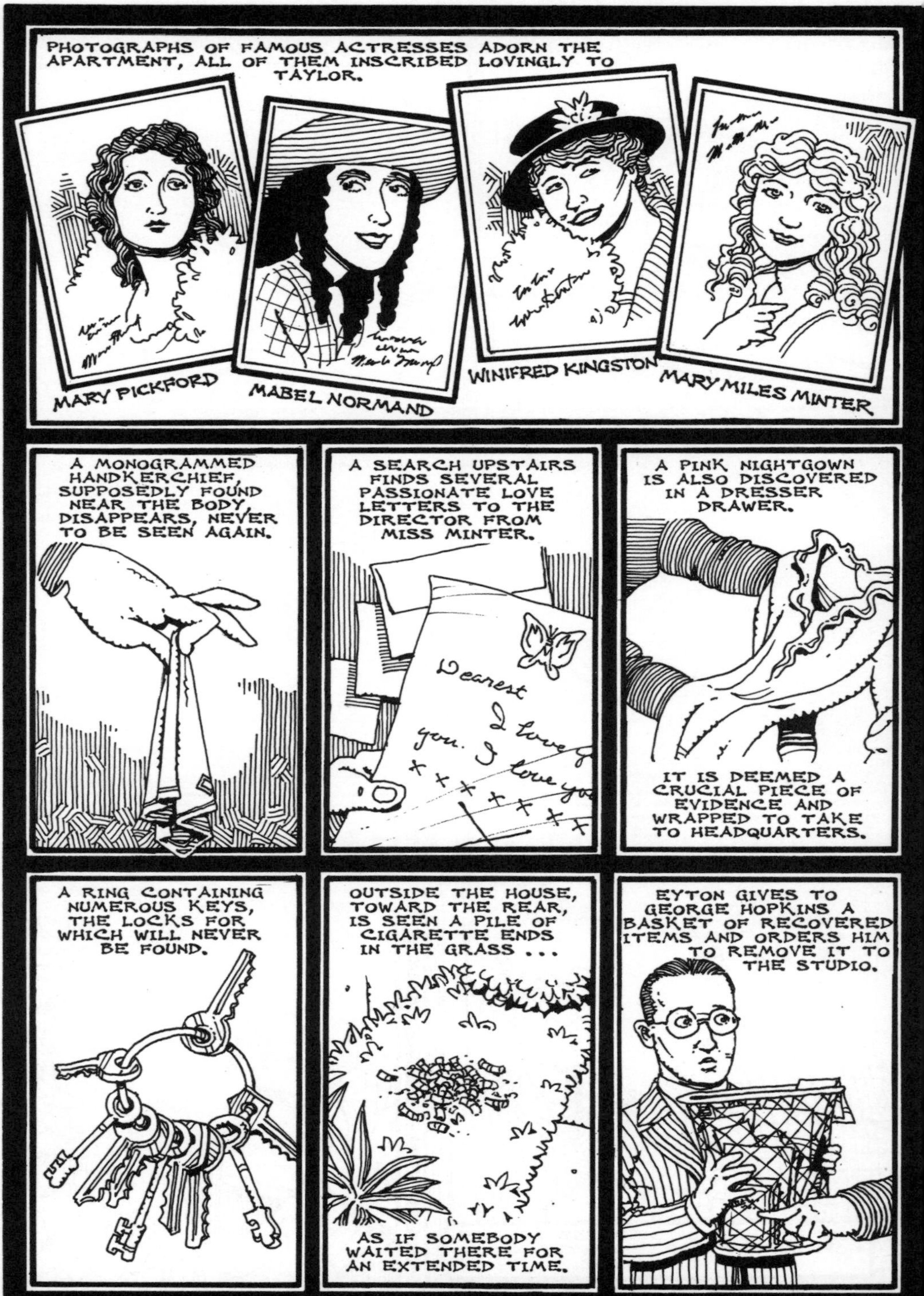
PHOTOGRAPHS OF FAMOUS ACTRESSES ADORN THE APARTMENT, ALL OF THEM INSCRIBED LOVINGLY TO TAYLOR.
MARY PICKFORD
MABEL NORMAND
WINIFRED KINGSTON
MARY MILES MINTER
A MONOGRAMMED HANDKERCHIEF, SUPPOSEDLY FOUND NEAR THE BODY, DISAPPEARS, NEVER TO BE SEEN AGAIN.
A SEARCH UPSTAIRS FINDS SEVERAL PASSIONATE LOVE LETTERS TO THE DIRECTOR FROM MISS MINTER.
Dearest
I love you. I love you
A PINK NIGHTGOWN IS ALSO DISCOVERED IN A DRESSER DRAWER.
IT IS DEEMED A CRUCIAL PIECE OF EVIDENCE AND WRAPPED TO TAKE TO HEADQUARTERS.
A RING CONTAINING NUMEROUS KEYS, THE LOCKS FOR WHICH WILL NEVER BE FOUND.
OUTSIDE THE HOUSE, TOWARD THE REAR, IS SEEN A PILE OF CIGARETTE ENDS IN THE GRASS . . .
AS IF SOMEBODY WAITED THERE FOR AN EXTENDED TIME.
EYTON GIVES TO GEORGE HOPKINS A BASKET OF RECOVERED ITEMS AND ORDERS HIM TO REMOVE IT TO THE STUDIO.

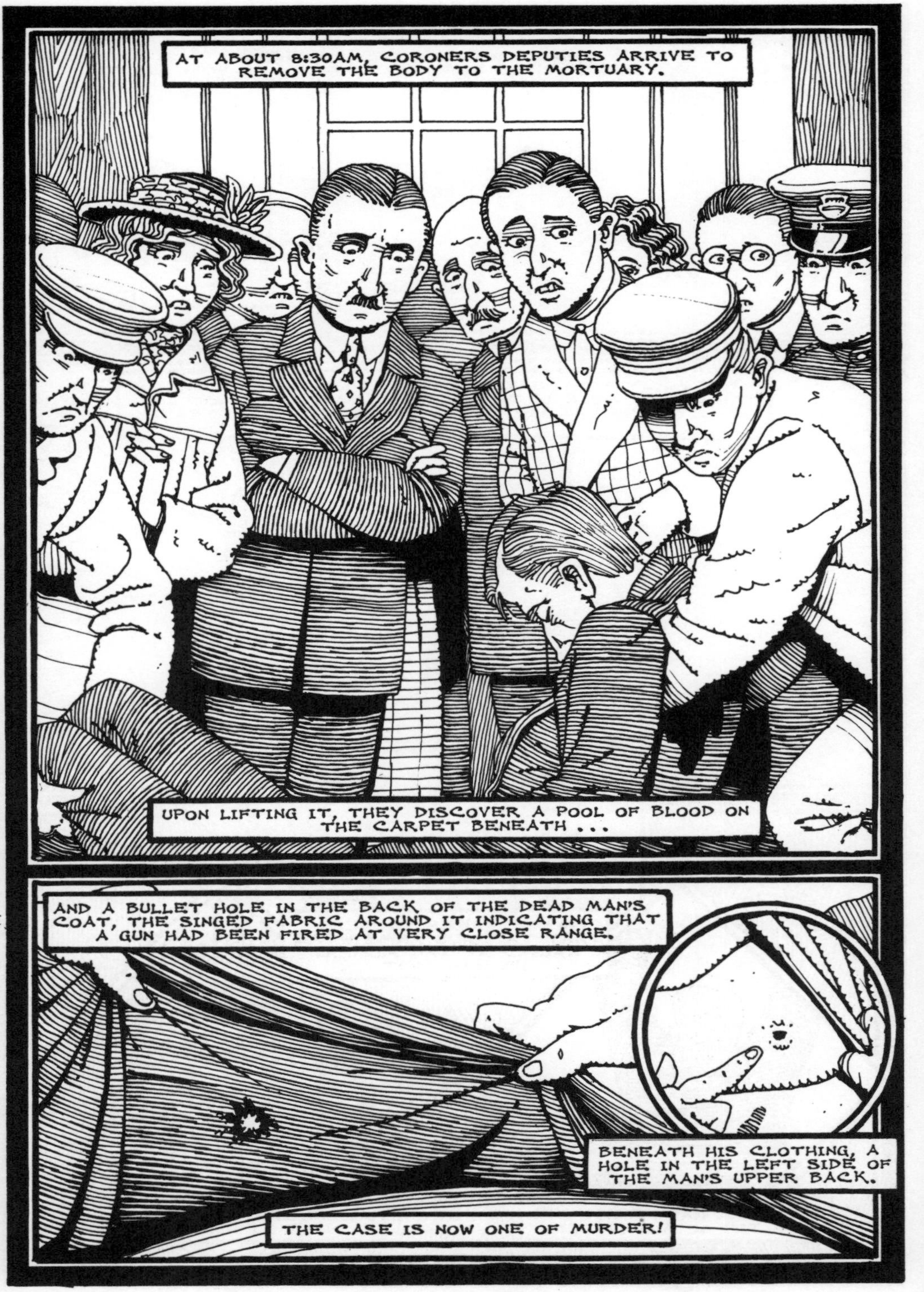
AT ABOUT 8:30AM, CORONERS DEPUTIES ARRIVE TO REMOVE THE BODY TO THE MORTUARY.
UPON LIFTING IT, THEY DISCOVER A POOL OF BLOOD ON THE CARPET BENEATH ...
AND A BULLET HOLE IN THE BACK OF THE DEAD MAN'S COAT, THE SINGED FABRIC AROUND IT INDICATING THAT A GUN HAD BEEN FIRED AT VERY CLOSE RANGE.
BENEATH HIS CLOTHING, A HOLE IN THE LEFT SIDE OF THE MAN'S UPPER BACK.
THE CASE IS NOW ONE OF MURDER!

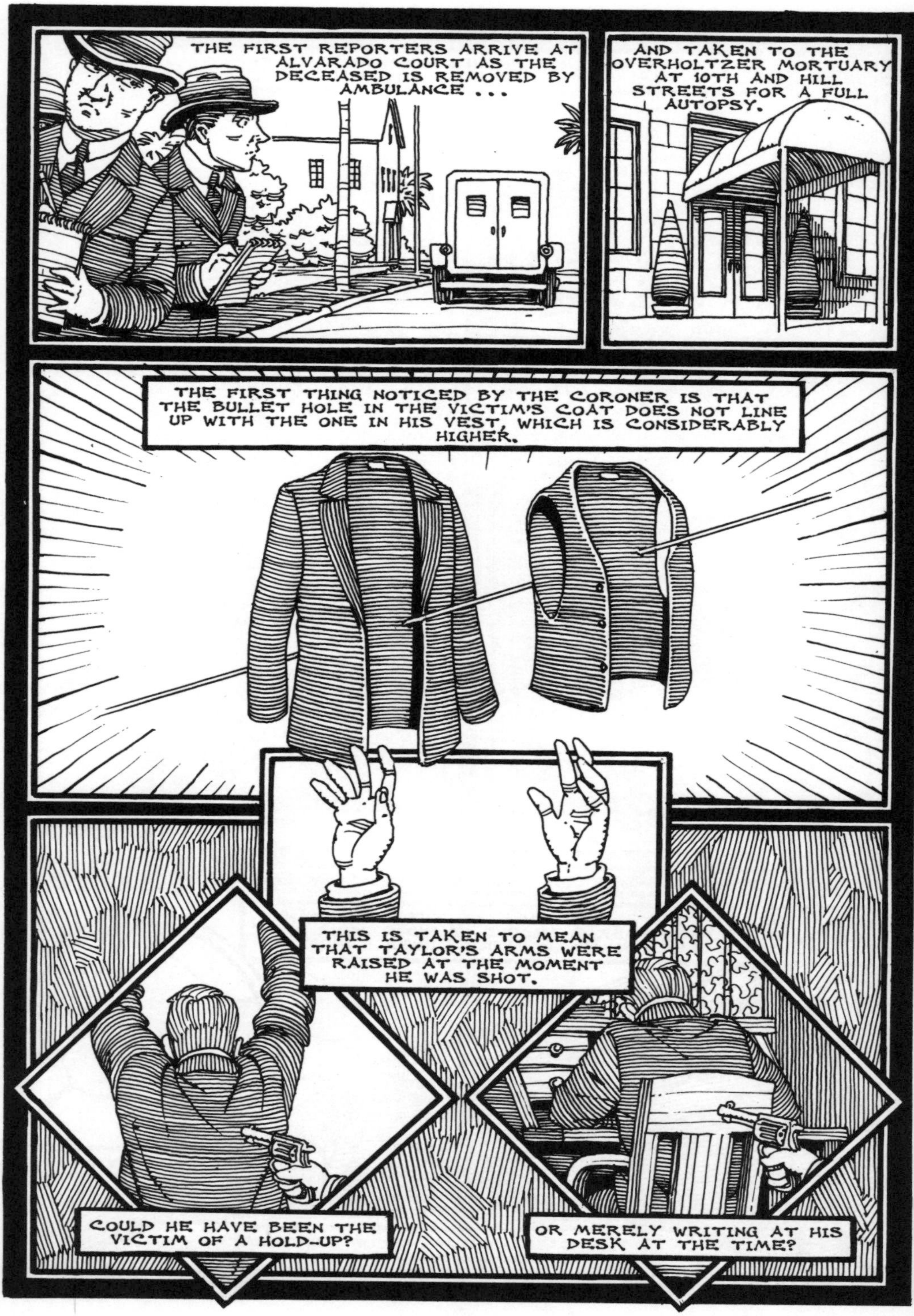
THE FIRST REPORTERS ARRIVE AT ALVARADO COURT AS THE DECEASED IS REMOVED BY AMBULANCE ...
AND TAKEN TO THE OVERHOLTZER MORTUARY AT 10TH AND HILL STREETS FOR A FULL AUTOPSY.
THE FIRST THING NOTICED BY THE CORONER IS THAT THE BULLET HOLE IN THE VICTIM'S COAT DOES NOT LINE UP WITH THE ONE IN HIS VEST, WHICH IS CONSIDERABLY HIGHER.
THIS IS TAKEN TO MEAN THAT TAYLOR'S ARMS WERE RAISED AT THE MOMENT HE WAS SHOT.
COULD HE HAVE BEEN THE VICTIM OF A HOLD-UP?
OR MERELY WRITING AT HIS DESK AT THE TIME?

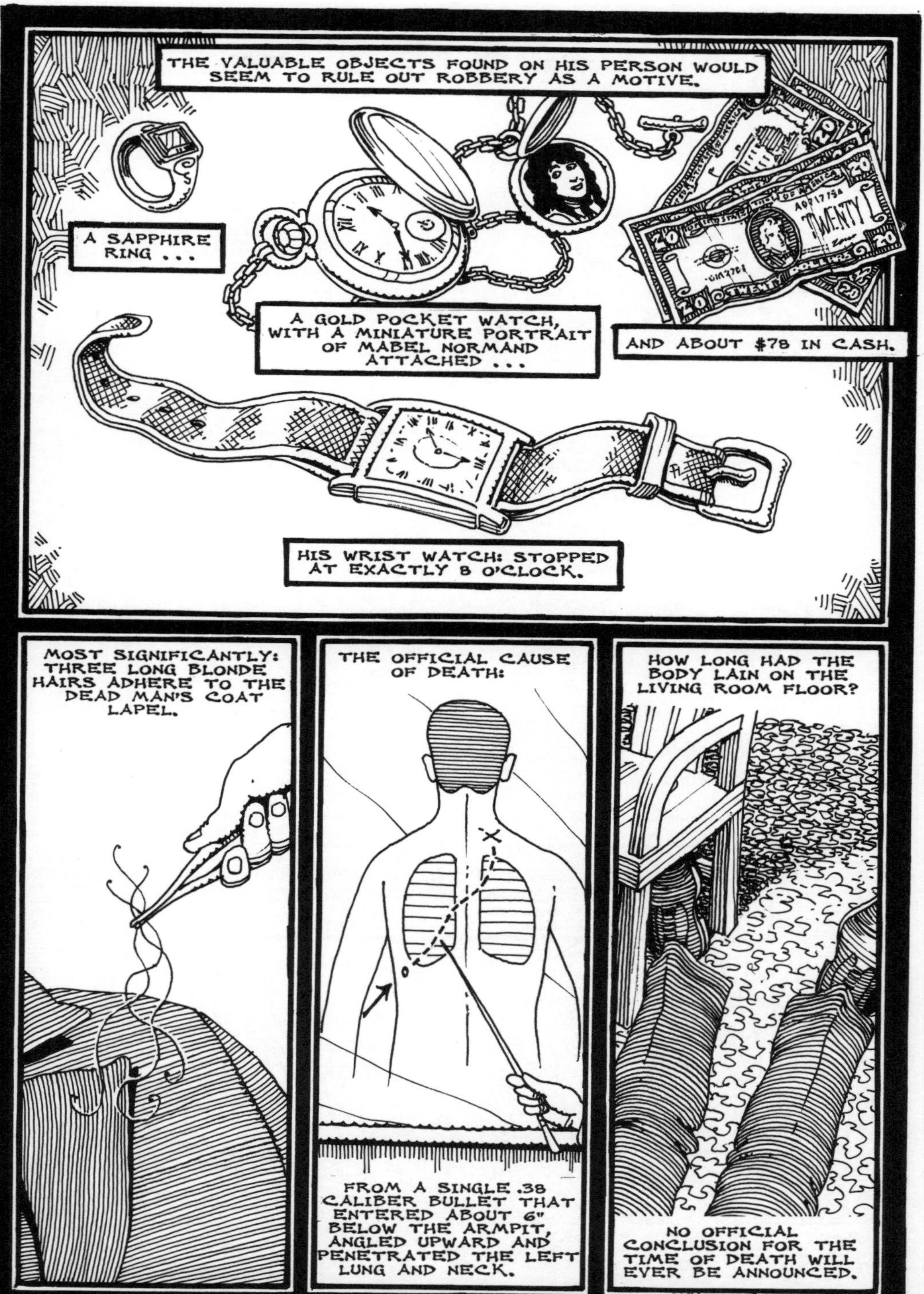
THE VALUABLE OBJECTS FOUND ON HIS PERSON WOULD SEEM TO RULE OUT ROBBERY AS A MOTIVE.
A SAPPHIRE RING ...
A GOLD POCKET WATCH, WITH A MINIATURE PORTRAIT OF MABEL NORMAND ATTACHED ...
AND ABOUT $78 IN CASH.
HIS WRIST WATCH: STOPPED AT EXACTLY 8 O'CLOCK.
MOST SIGNIFICANTLY: THREE LONG BLONDE HAIRS ADHERE TO THE DEAD MAN'S COAT LAPEL.
THE OFFICIAL CAUSE OF DEATH:
FROM A SINGLE .38 CALIBER BULLET THAT ENTERED ABOUT 6" BELOW THE ARMPIT, ANGLED UPWARD AND PENETRATED THE LEFT LUNG AND NECK.
HOW LONG HAD THE BODY LAIN ON THE LIVING ROOM FLOOR?
NO OFFICIAL CONCLUSION FOR THE TIME OF DEATH WILL EVER BE ANNOUNCED.

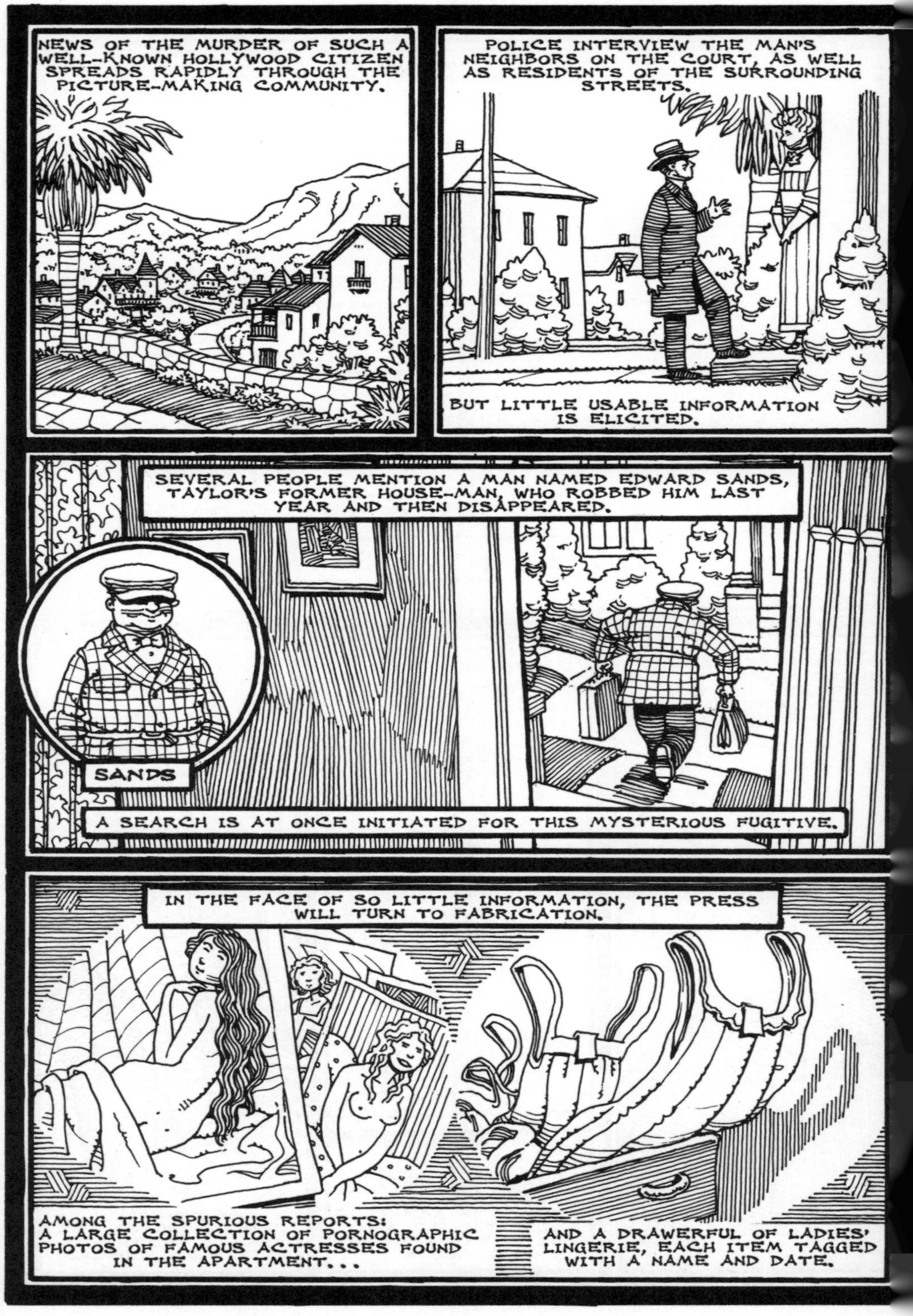
NEWS OF THE MURDER OF SUCH A WELL-KNOWN HOLLYWOOD CITIZEN SPREADS RAPIDLY THROUGH THE PICTURE-MAKING COMMUNITY.
POLICE INTERVIEW THE MAN'S NEIGHBORS ON THE COURT, AS WELL AS RESIDENTS OF THE SURROUNDING STREETS.
BUT LITTLE USABLE INFORMATION IS ELICITED.
SEVERAL PEOPLE MENTION A MAN NAMED EDWARD SANDS, TAYLOR'S FORMER HOUSE-MAN, WHO ROBBED HIM LAST YEAR AND THEN DISAPPEARED.
SANDS
A SEARCH IS AT ONCE INITIATED FOR THIS MYSTERIOUS FUGITIVE.
IN THE FACE OF SO LITTLE INFORMATION, THE PRESS WILL TURN TO FABRICATION.
AMONG THE SPURIOUS REPORTS: A LARGE COLLECTION OF PORNOGRAPHIC PHOTOS OF FAMOUS ACTRESSES FOUND IN THE APARTMENT...
AND A DRAWERFUL OF LADIES' LINGERIE, EACH ITEM TAGGED WITH A NAME AND DATE.

PART III

THE FATAL NIGHT

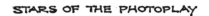

STARS OF THE PHOTOPLAY

DOUGLAS FAIRBANKS

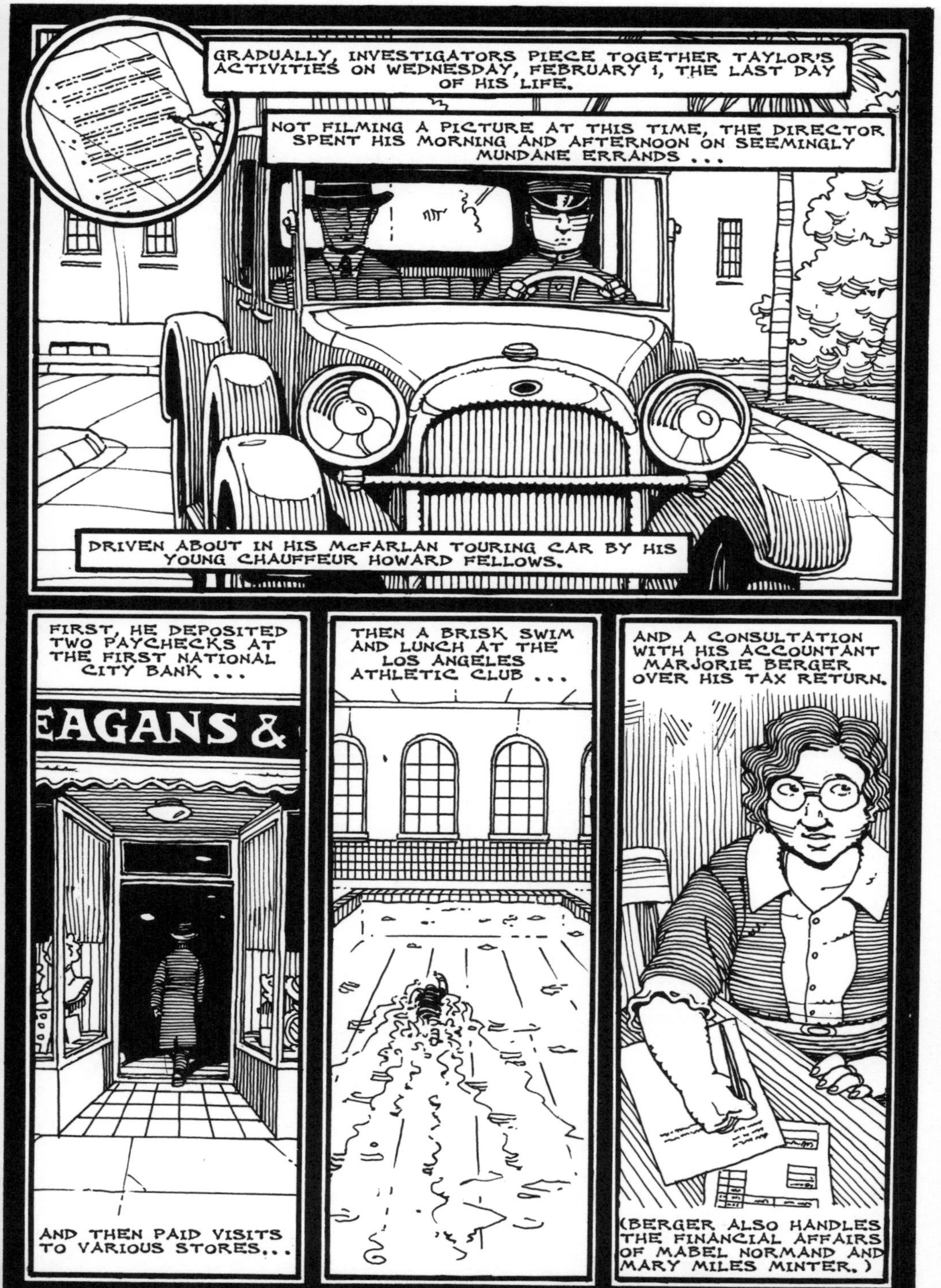
GRADUALLY, INVESTIGATORS PIECE TOGETHER TAYLOR'S ACTIVITIES ON WEDNESDAY, FEBRUARY 1, THE LAST DAY OF HIS LIFE.
NOT FILMING A PICTURE AT THIS TIME, THE DIRECTOR SPENT HIS MORNING AND AFTERNOON ON SEEMINGLY MUNDANE ERRANDS ...
DRIVEN ABOUT IN HIS McFARLAN TOURING CAR BY HIS YOUNG CHAUFFEUR HOWARD FELLOWS.
FIRST, HE DEPOSITED TWO PAYCHECKS AT THE FIRST NATIONAL CITY BANK ...
EAGANS &
AND THEN PAID VISITS TO VARIOUS STORES...
THEN A BRISK SWIM AND LUNCH AT THE LOS ANGELES ATHLETIC CLUB ...
AND A CONSULTATION WITH HIS ACCOUNTANT MARJORIE BERGER OVER HIS TAX RETURN.
(BERGER ALSO HANDLES THE FINANCIAL AFFAIRS OF MABEL NORMAND AND MARY MILES MINTER.)

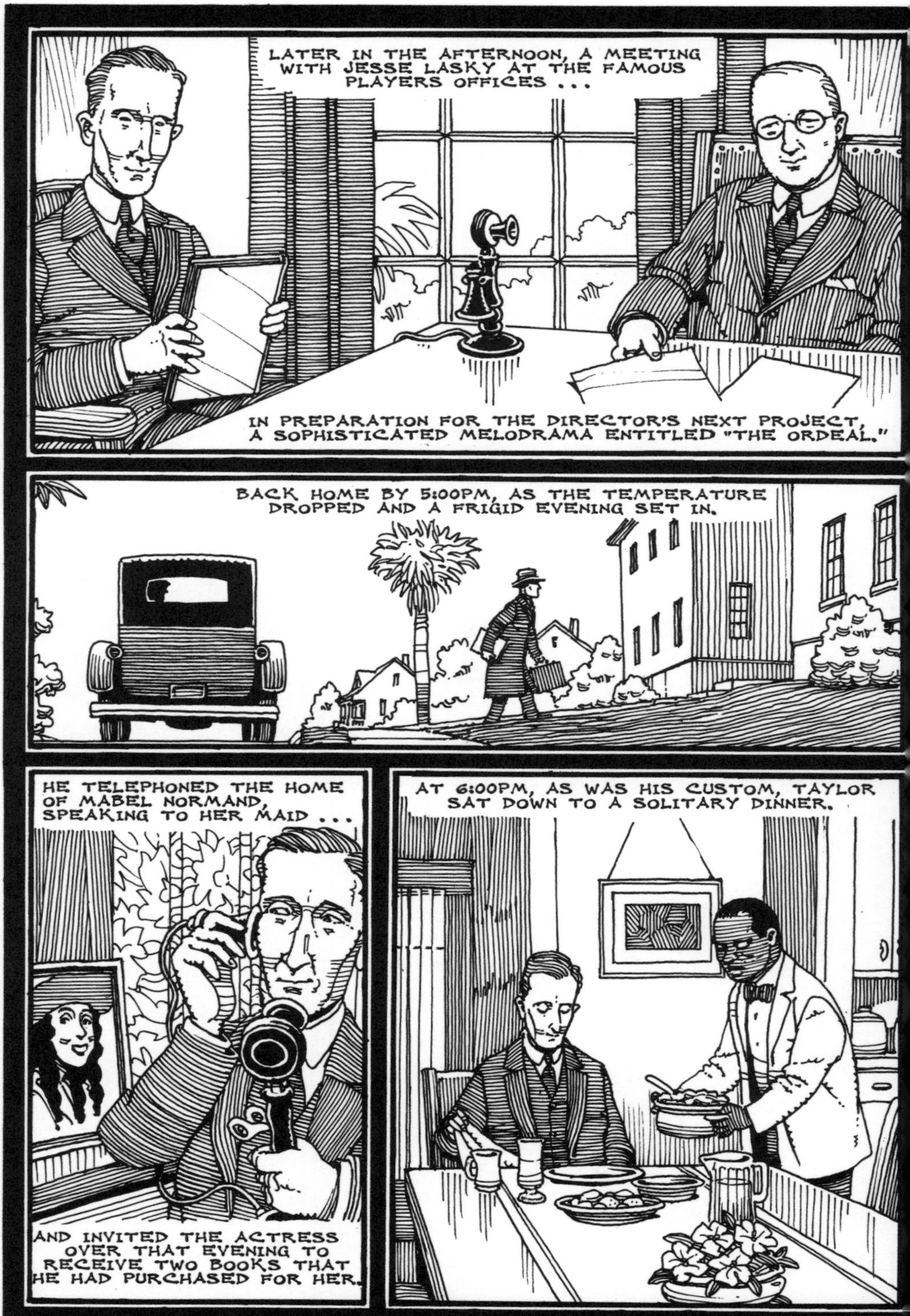
LATER IN THE AFTERNOON, A MEETING WITH JESSE LASKY AT THE FAMOUS PLAYERS OFFICES ...
IN PREPARATION FOR THE DIRECTOR'S NEXT PROJECT, A SOPHISTICATED MELODRAMA ENTITLED "THE ORDEAL."
BACK HOME BY 5:00PM, AS THE TEMPERATURE DROPPED AND A FRIGID EVENING SET IN.
HE TELEPHONED THE HOME OF MABEL NORMAND, SPEAKING TO HER MAID ...
AND INVITED THE ACTRESS OVER THAT EVENING TO RECEIVE TWO BOOKS THAT HE HAD PURCHASED FOR HER.
AT 6:00PM, AS WAS HIS CUSTOM, TAYLOR SAT DOWN TO A SOLITARY DINNER.

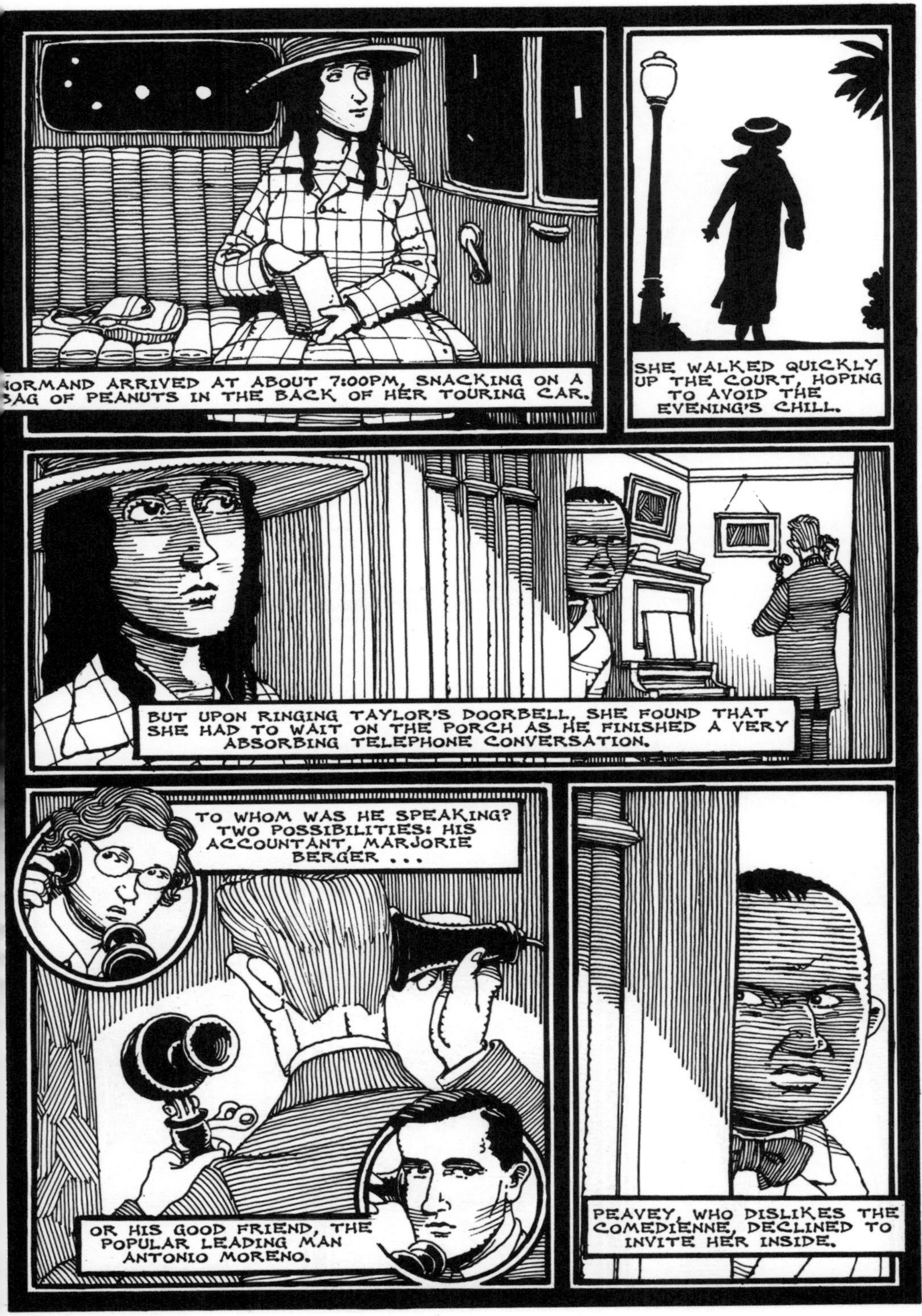
NORMAND ARRIVED AT ABOUT 7:00PM, SNACKING ON A BAG OF PEANUTS IN THE BACK OF HER TOURING CAR.
SHE WALKED QUICKLY UP THE COURT, HOPING TO AVOID THE EVENING'S CHILL.
BUT UPON RINGING TAYLOR'S DOORBELL, SHE FOUND THAT SHE HAD TO WAIT ON THE PORCH AS HE FINISHED A VERY ABSORBING TELEPHONE CONVERSATION.
TO WHOM WAS HE SPEAKING? TWO POSSIBILITIES: HIS ACCOUNTANT, MARJORIE BERGER ...
OR HIS GOOD FRIEND, THE POPULAR LEADING MAN ANTONIO MORENO.
PEAVEY, WHO DISLIKES THE COMEDIENNE, DECLINED TO INVITE HER INSIDE.

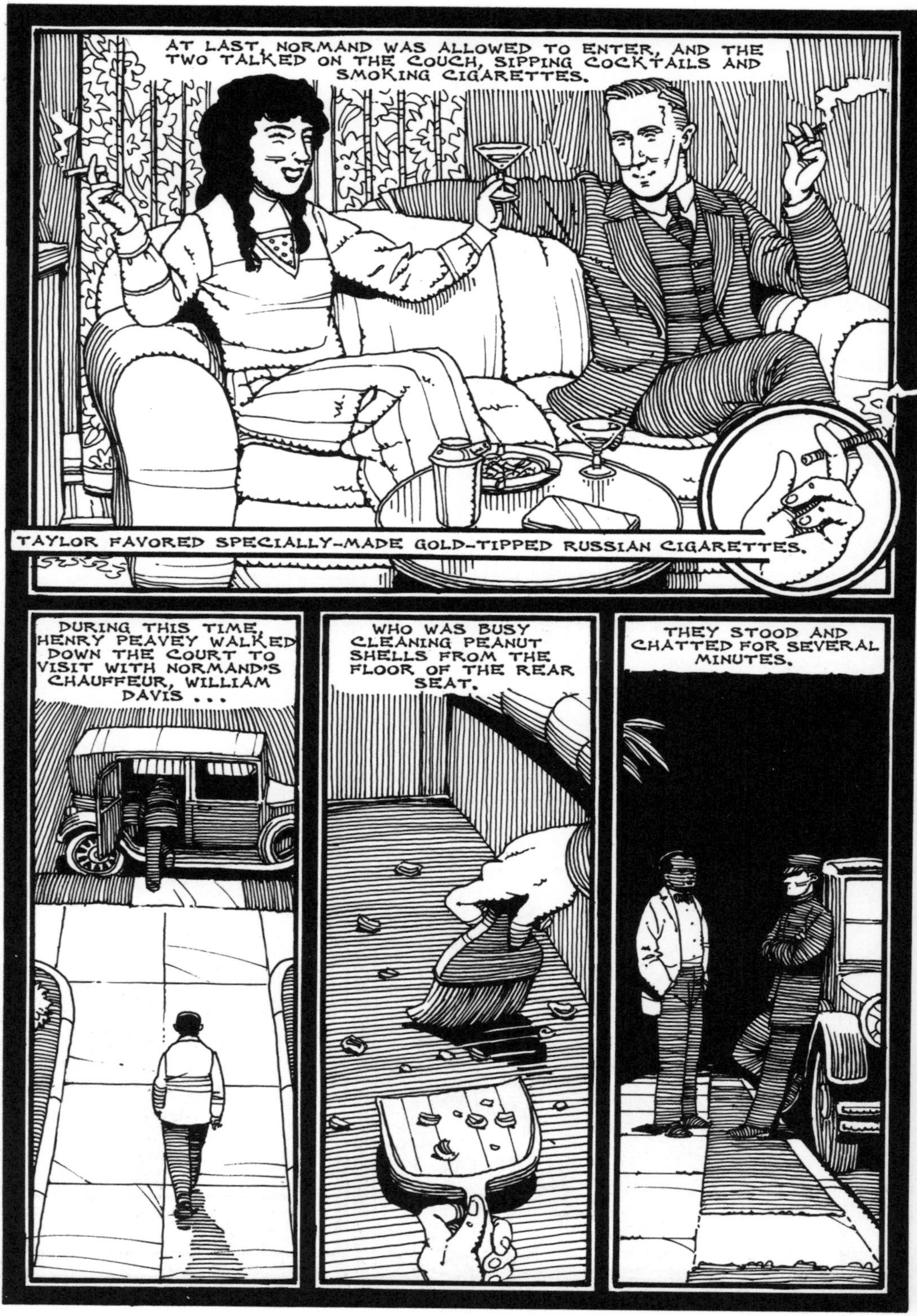
AT LAST, NORMAND WAS ALLOWED TO ENTER, AND THE TWO TALKED ON THE COUCH, SIPPING COCKTAILS AND SMOKING CIGARETTES.
TAYLOR FAVORED SPECIALLY-MADE GOLD-TIPPED RUSSIAN CIGARETTES.
DURING THIS TIME, HENRY PEAVEY WALKED DOWN THE COURT TO VISIT WITH NORMAND'S CHAUFFEUR, WILLIAM DAVIS . . .
WHO WAS BUSY CLEANING PEANUT SHELLS FROM THE FLOOR OF THE REAR SEAT.
THEY STOOD AND CHATTED FOR SEVERAL MINUTES.

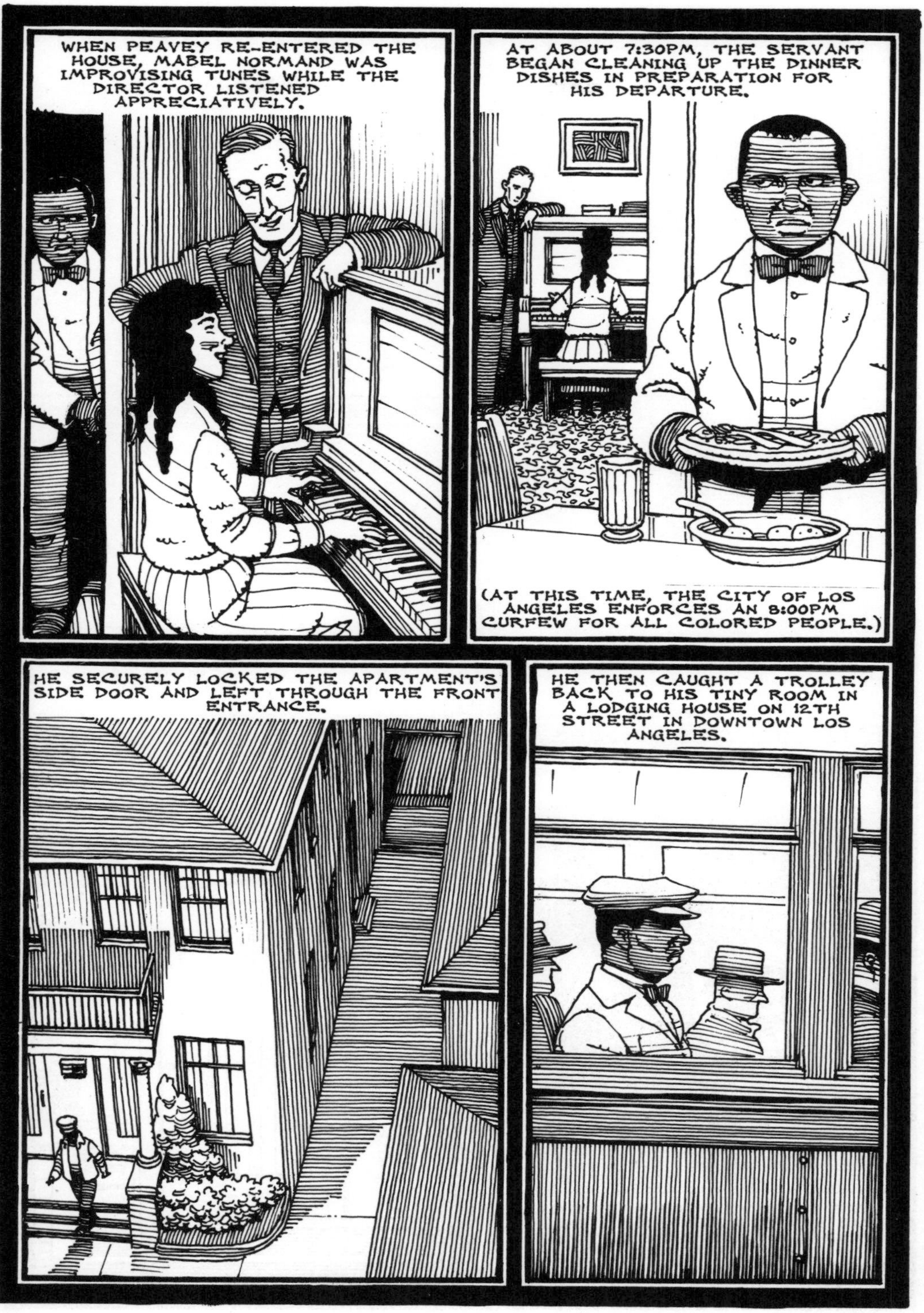
WHEN PEAVEY RE-ENTERED THE HOUSE, MABEL NORMAND WAS IMPROVISING TUNES WHILE THE DIRECTOR LISTENED APPRECIATIVELY.
AT ABOUT 7:30PM, THE SERVANT BEGAN CLEANING UP THE DINNER DISHES IN PREPARATION FOR HIS DEPARTURE.
(AT THIS TIME, THE CITY OF LOS ANGELES ENFORCES AN 8:00PM CURFEW FOR ALL COLORED PEOPLE.)
HE SECURELY LOCKED THE APARTMENT'S SIDE DOOR AND LEFT THROUGH THE FRONT ENTRANCE.
HE THEN CAUGHT A TROLLEY BACK TO HIS TINY ROOM IN A LODGING HOUSE ON 12TH STREET IN DOWNTOWN LOS ANGELES.

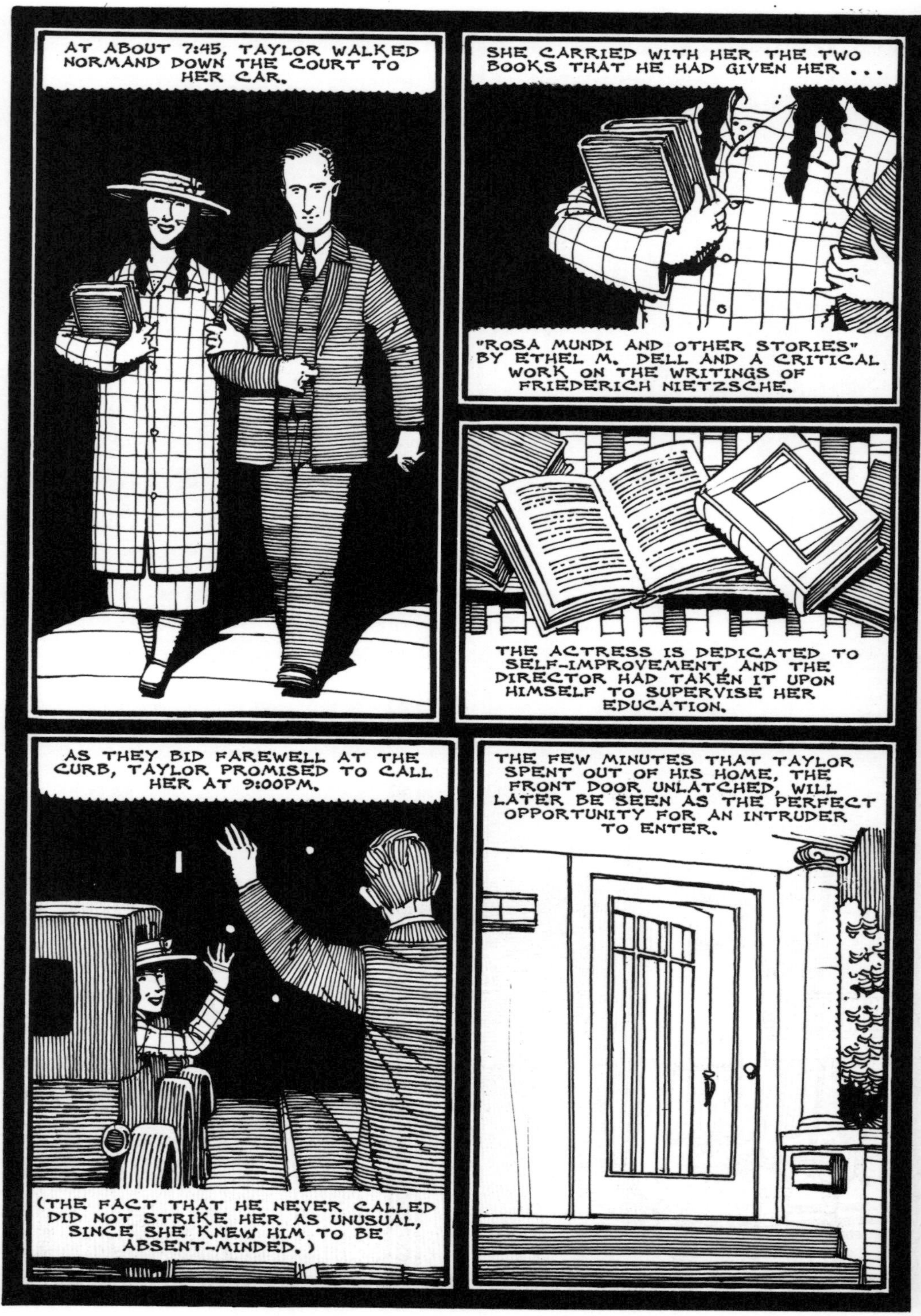
AT ABOUT 7:45, TAYLOR WALKED NORMAND DOWN THE COURT TO HER CAR.
SHE CARRIED WITH HER THE TWO BOOKS THAT HE HAD GIVEN HER ...
"ROSA MUNDI AND OTHER STORIES" BY ETHEL M. DELL AND A CRITICAL WORK ON THE WRITINGS OF FRIEDERICH NIETZSCHE.
THE ACTRESS IS DEDICATED TO SELF-IMPROVEMENT, AND THE DIRECTOR HAD TAKEN IT UPON HIMSELF TO SUPERVISE HER EDUCATION.
AS THEY BID FAREWELL AT THE CURB, TAYLOR PROMISED TO CALL HER AT 9:00PM.
(THE FACT THAT HE NEVER CALLED DID NOT STRIKE HER AS UNUSUAL, SINCE SHE KNEW HIM TO BE ABSENT-MINDED.)
THE FEW MINUTES THAT TAYLOR SPENT OUT OF HIS HOME, THE FRONT DOOR UNLATCHED, WILL LATER BE SEEN AS THE PERFECT OPPORTUNITY FOR AN INTRUDER TO ENTER.

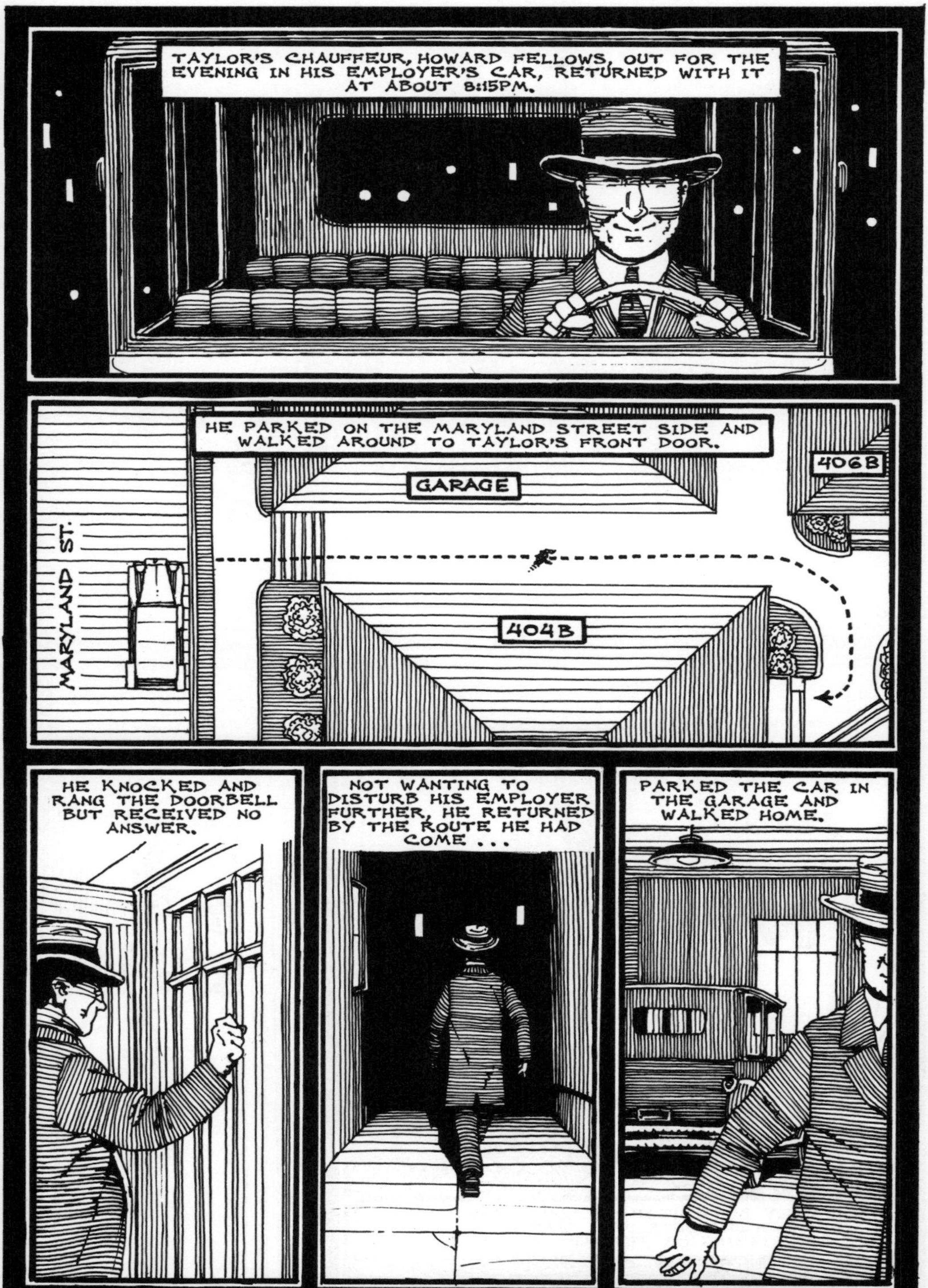
TAYLOR'S CHAUFFEUR, HOWARD FELLOWS, OUT FOR THE EVENING IN HIS EMPLOYER'S CAR, RETURNED WITH IT AT ABOUT 8:15PM.
HE PARKED ON THE MARYLAND STREET SIDE AND WALKED AROUND TO TAYLOR'S FRONT DOOR.
GARAGE
406B
MARYLAND ST.
404B
HE KNOCKED AND RANG THE DOORBELL BUT RECEIVED NO ANSWER.
NOT WANTING TO DISTURB HIS EMPLOYER FURTHER, HE RETURNED BY THE ROUTE HE HAD COME ...
PARKED THE CAR IN THE GARAGE AND WALKED HOME.

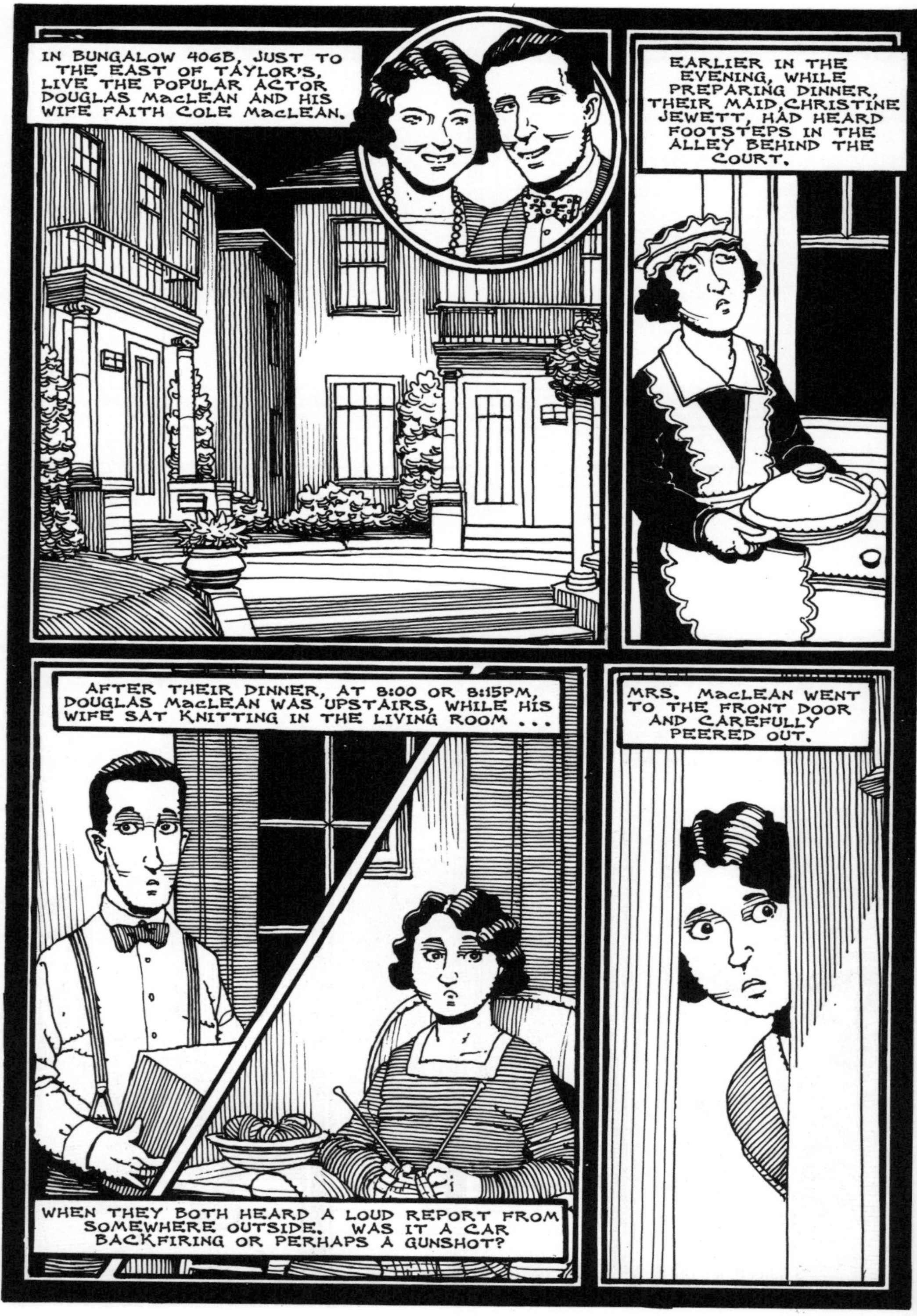
IN BUNGALOW 406B, JUST TO THE EAST OF TAYLOR'S, LIVE THE POPULAR ACTOR DOUGLAS MacLEAN AND HIS WIFE FAITH COLE MacLEAN.
EARLIER IN THE EVENING, WHILE PREPARING DINNER, THEIR MAID, CHRISTINE JEWETT, HAD HEARD FOOTSTEPS IN THE ALLEY BEHIND THE COURT.
AFTER THEIR DINNER, AT 8:00 OR 8:15PM, DOUGLAS MacLEAN WAS UPSTAIRS, WHILE HIS WIFE SAT KNITTING IN THE LIVING ROOM ...
WHEN THEY BOTH HEARD A LOUD REPORT FROM SOMEWHERE OUTSIDE. WAS IT A CAR BACKFIRING OR PERHAPS A GUNSHOT?
MRS. MacLEAN WENT TO THE FRONT DOOR AND CAREFULLY PEERED OUT.

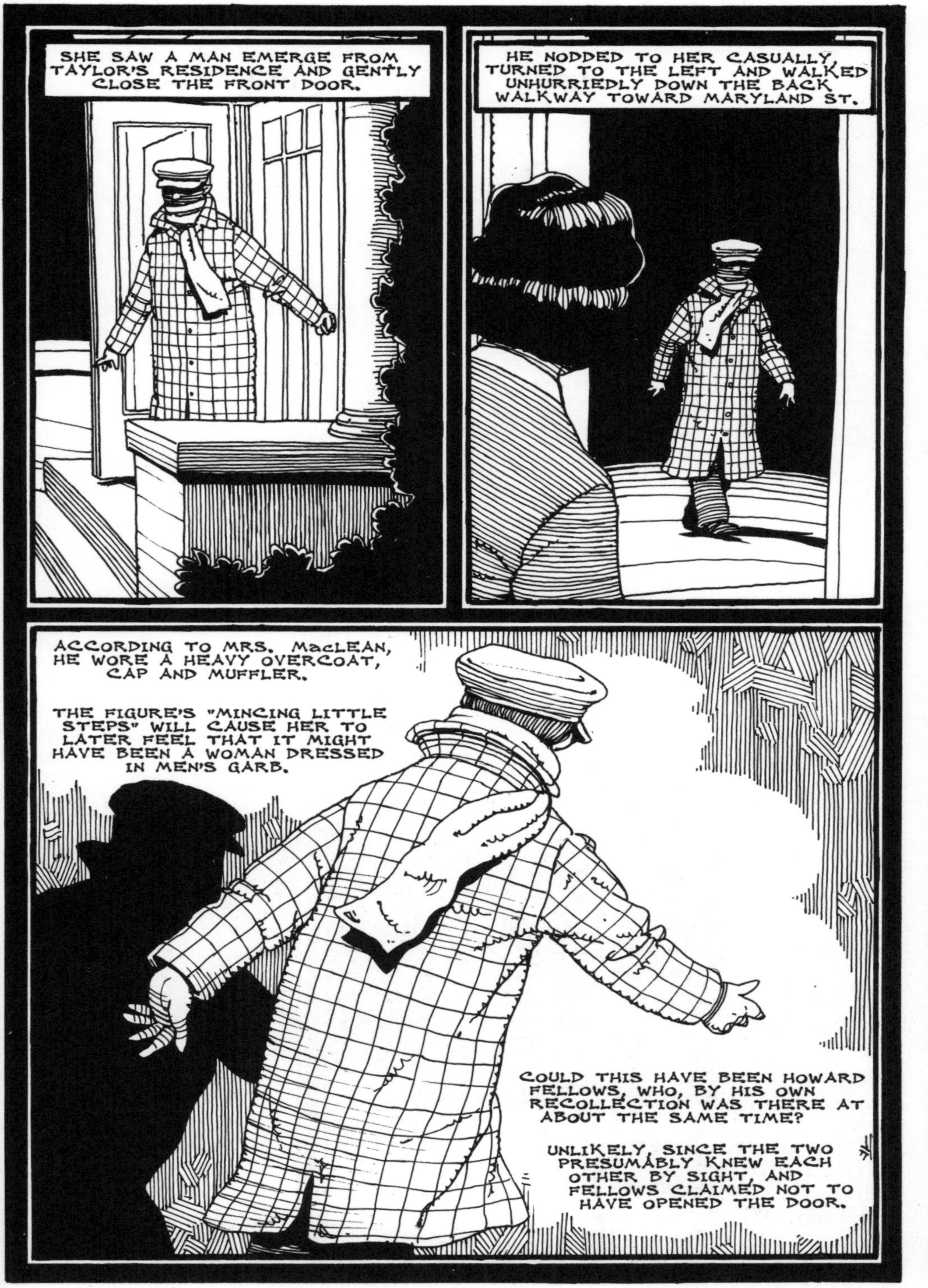
SHE SAW A MAN EMERGE FROM TAYLOR'S RESIDENCE AND GENTLY CLOSE THE FRONT DOOR.
HE NODDED TO HER CASUALLY, TURNED TO THE LEFT AND WALKED UNHURRIEDLY DOWN THE BACK WALKWAY TOWARD MARYLAND ST.
ACCORDING TO MRS. MacLEAN, HE WORE A HEAVY OVERCOAT, CAP AND MUFFLER.
THE FIGURE'S "MINCING LITTLE STEPS" WILL CAUSE HER TO LATER FEEL THAT IT MIGHT HAVE BEEN A WOMAN DRESSED IN MEN'S GARB.
COULD THIS HAVE BEEN HOWARD FELLOWS, WHO, BY HIS OWN RECOLLECTION WAS THERE AT ABOUT THE SAME TIME?
UNLIKELY, SINCE THE TWO PRESUMABLY KNEW EACH OTHER BY SIGHT, AND FELLOWS CLAIMED NOT TO HAVE OPENED THE DOOR.

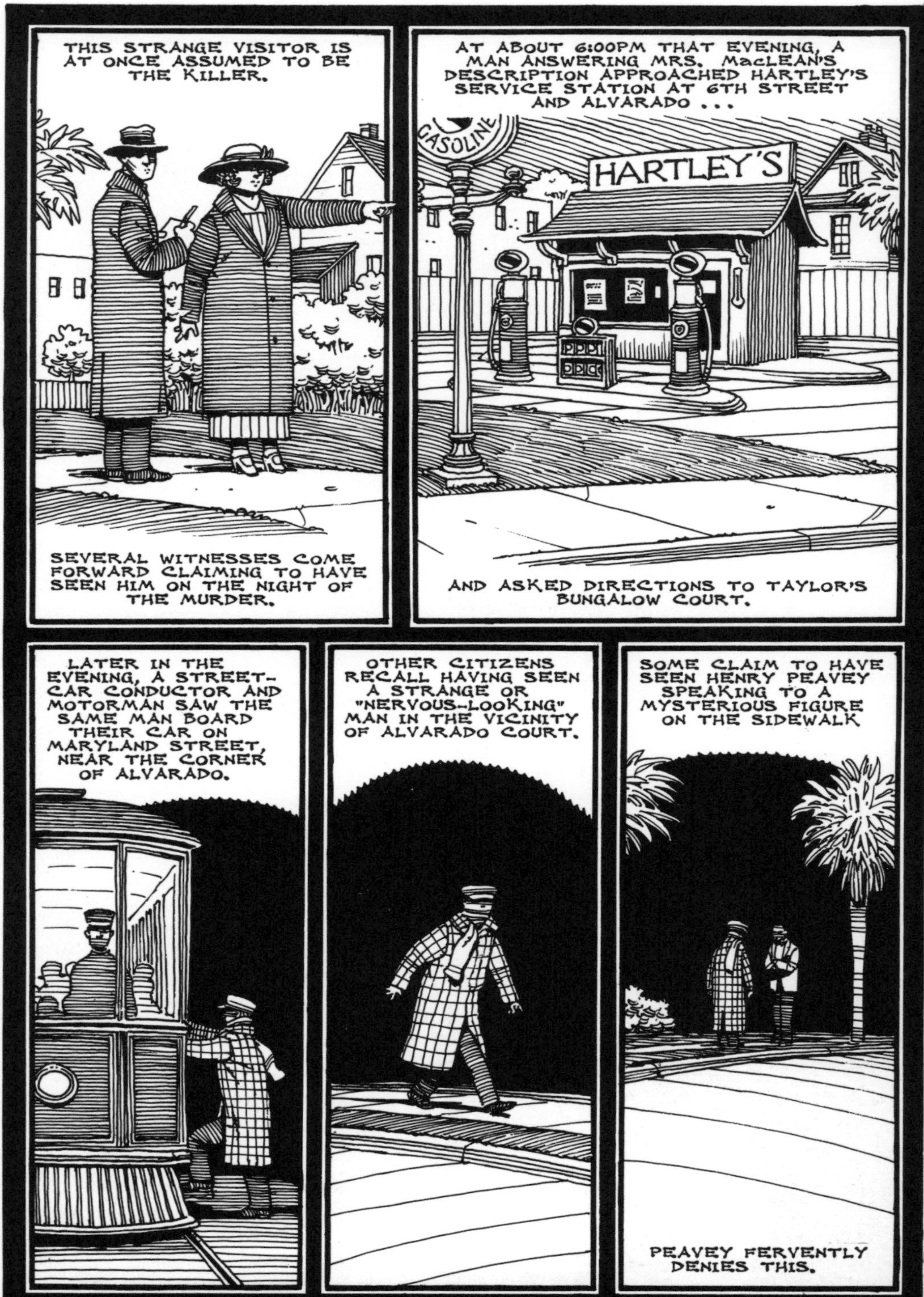
THIS STRANGE VISITOR IS AT ONCE ASSUMED TO BE THE KILLER.
SEVERAL WITNESSES COME FORWARD CLAIMING TO HAVE SEEN HIM ON THE NIGHT OF THE MURDER.
AT ABOUT 6:00PM THAT EVENING, A MAN ANSWERING MRS. MacLEAN'S DESCRIPTION APPROACHED HARTLEY'S SERVICE STATION AT 6TH STREET AND ALVARADO ...
GASOLINE
HARTLEY'S
AND ASKED DIRECTIONS TO TAYLOR'S BUNGALOW COURT.
LATER IN THE EVENING, A STREET-CAR CONDUCTOR AND MOTORMAN SAW THE SAME MAN BOARD THEIR CAR ON MARYLAND STREET, NEAR THE CORNER OF ALVARADO.
OTHER CITIZENS RECALL HAVING SEEN A STRANGE OR "NERVOUS-LOOKING" MAN IN THE VICINITY OF ALVARADO COURT.
SOME CLAIM TO HAVE SEEN HENRY PEAVEY SPEAKING TO A MYSTERIOUS FIGURE ON THE SIDEWALK
PEAVEY FERVENTLY DENIES THIS.

PART IV

WHO WAS
WILLIAM DESMOND TAYLOR?

STARS OF THE PHOTOPLAY

THEDA BARA

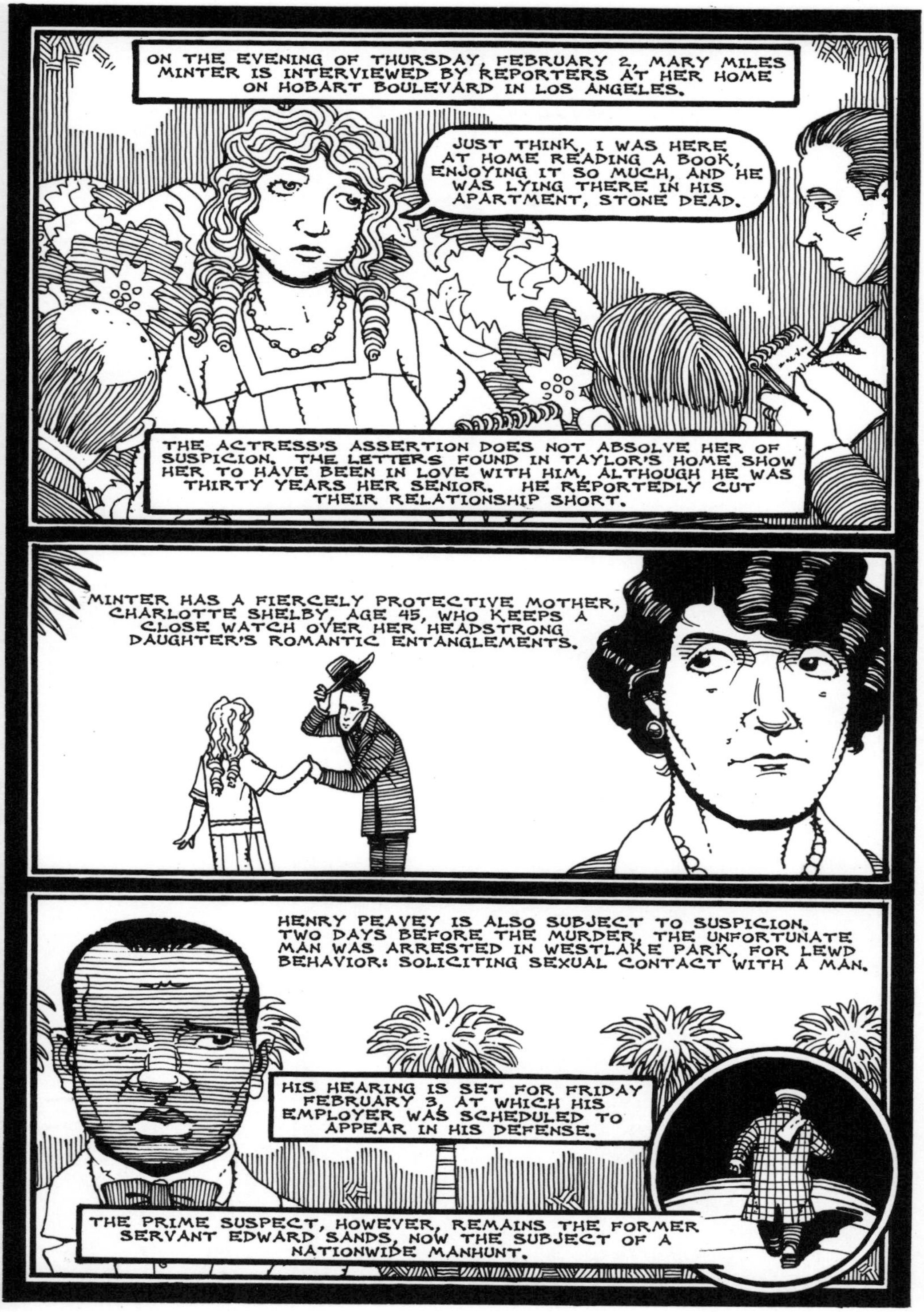
ON THE EVENING OF THURSDAY, FEBRUARY 2, MARY MILES MINTER IS INTERVIEWED BY REPORTERS AT HER HOME ON HOBART BOULEVARD IN LOS ANGELES.
JUST THINK, I WAS HERE AT HOME READING A BOOK, ENJOYING IT SO MUCH, AND HE WAS LYING THERE IN HIS APARTMENT, STONE DEAD.
THE ACTRESS'S ASSERTION DOES NOT ABSOLVE HER OF SUSPICION. THE LETTERS FOUND IN TAYLOR'S HOME SHOW HER TO HAVE BEEN IN LOVE WITH HIM, ALTHOUGH HE WAS THIRTY YEARS HER SENIOR. HE REPORTEDLY CUT THEIR RELATIONSHIP SHORT.
MINTER HAS A FIERCELY PROTECTIVE MOTHER, CHARLOTTE SHELBY, AGE 45, WHO KEEPS A CLOSE WATCH OVER HER HEADSTRONG DAUGHTER'S ROMANTIC ENTANGLEMENTS.
HENRY PEAVEY IS ALSO SUBJECT TO SUSPICION. TWO DAYS BEFORE THE MURDER, THE UNFORTUNATE MAN WAS ARRESTED IN WESTLAKE PARK, FOR LEWD BEHAVIOR: SOLICITING SEXUAL CONTACT WITH A MAN.
HIS HEARING IS SET FOR FRIDAY FEBRUARY 3, AT WHICH HIS EMPLOYER WAS SCHEDULED TO APPEAR IN HIS DEFENSE.
THE PRIME SUSPECT, HOWEVER, REMAINS THE FORMER SERVANT EDWARD SANDS, NOW THE SUBJECT OF A NATIONWIDE MANHUNT.

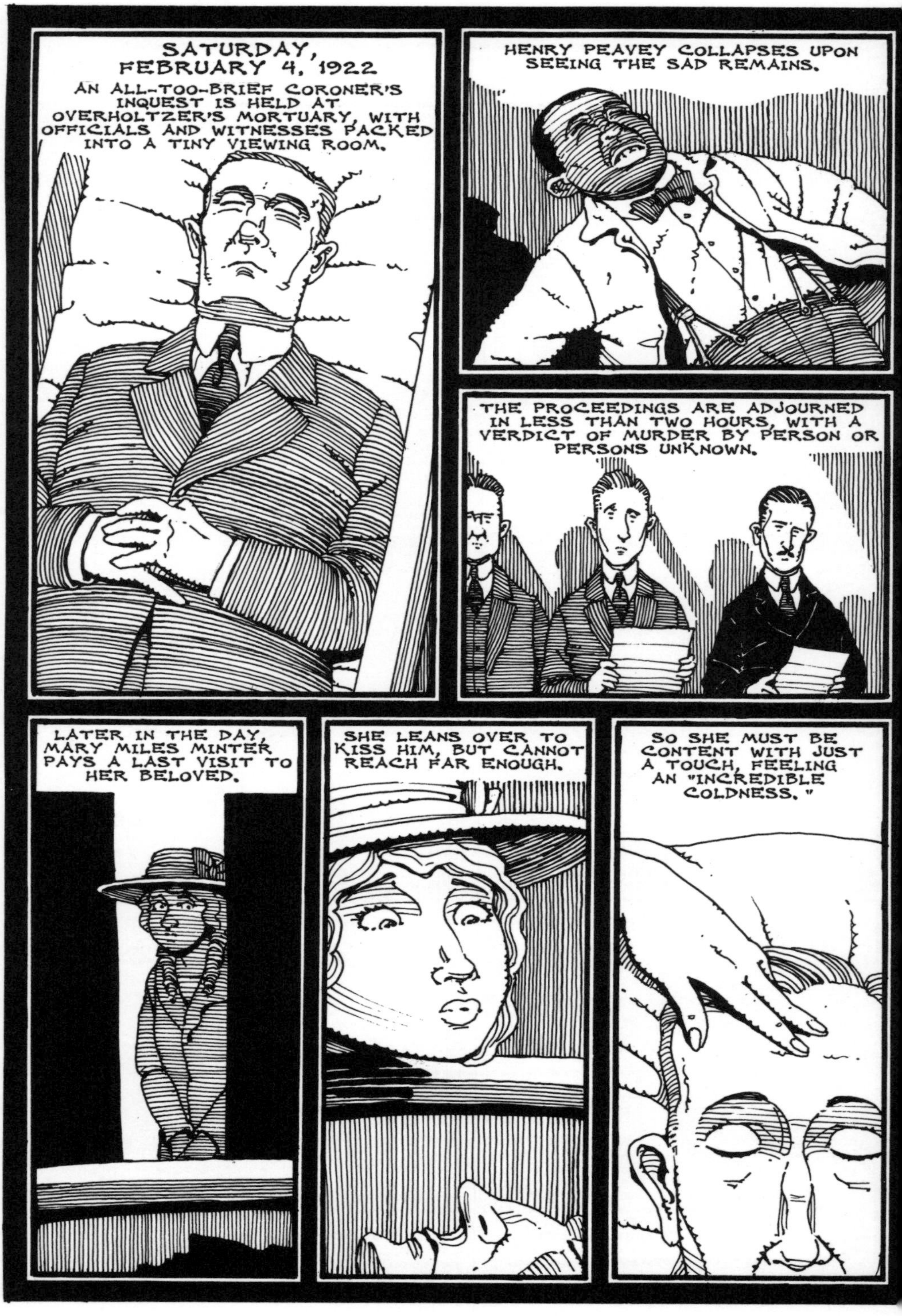
SATURDAY, FEBRUARY 4, 1922
AN ALL-TOO-BRIEF CORONER'S INQUEST IS HELD AT OVERHOLTZER'S MORTUARY, WITH OFFICIALS AND WITNESSES PACKED INTO A TINY VIEWING ROOM.
HENRY PEAVEY COLLAPSES UPON SEEING THE SAD REMAINS.
THE PROCEEDINGS ARE ADJOURNED IN LESS THAN TWO HOURS, WITH A VERDICT OF MURDER BY PERSON OR PERSONS UNKNOWN.
LATER IN THE DAY, MARY MILES MINTER PAYS A LAST VISIT TO HER BELOVED.
SHE LEANS OVER TO KISS HIM, BUT CANNOT REACH FAR ENOUGH.
SO SHE MUST BE CONTENT WITH JUST A TOUCH, FEELING AN "INCREDIBLE COLDNESS."

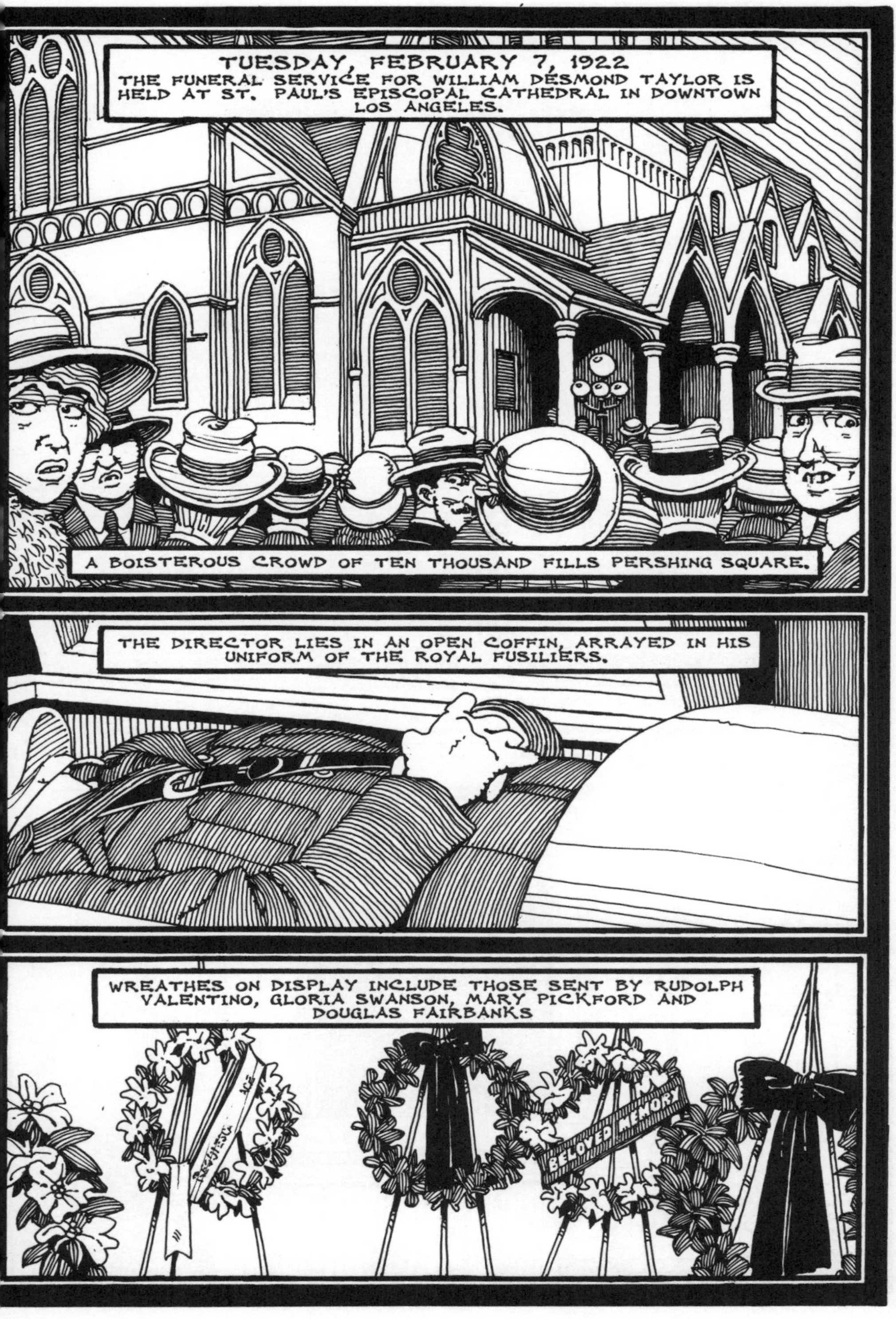
TUESDAY, FEBRUARY 7, 1922
THE FUNERAL SERVICE FOR WILLIAM DESMOND TAYLOR IS HELD AT ST. PAUL'S EPISCOPAL CATHEDRAL IN DOWNTOWN LOS ANGELES.
A BOISTEROUS CROWD OF TEN THOUSAND FILLS PERSHING SQUARE.
THE DIRECTOR LIES IN AN OPEN COFFIN, ARRAYED IN HIS UNIFORM OF THE ROYAL FUSILIERS.
WREATHES ON DISPLAY INCLUDE THOSE SENT BY RUDOLPH VALENTINO, GLORIA SWANSON, MARY PICKFORD AND DOUGLAS FAIRBANKS
BELOVED MEMORY

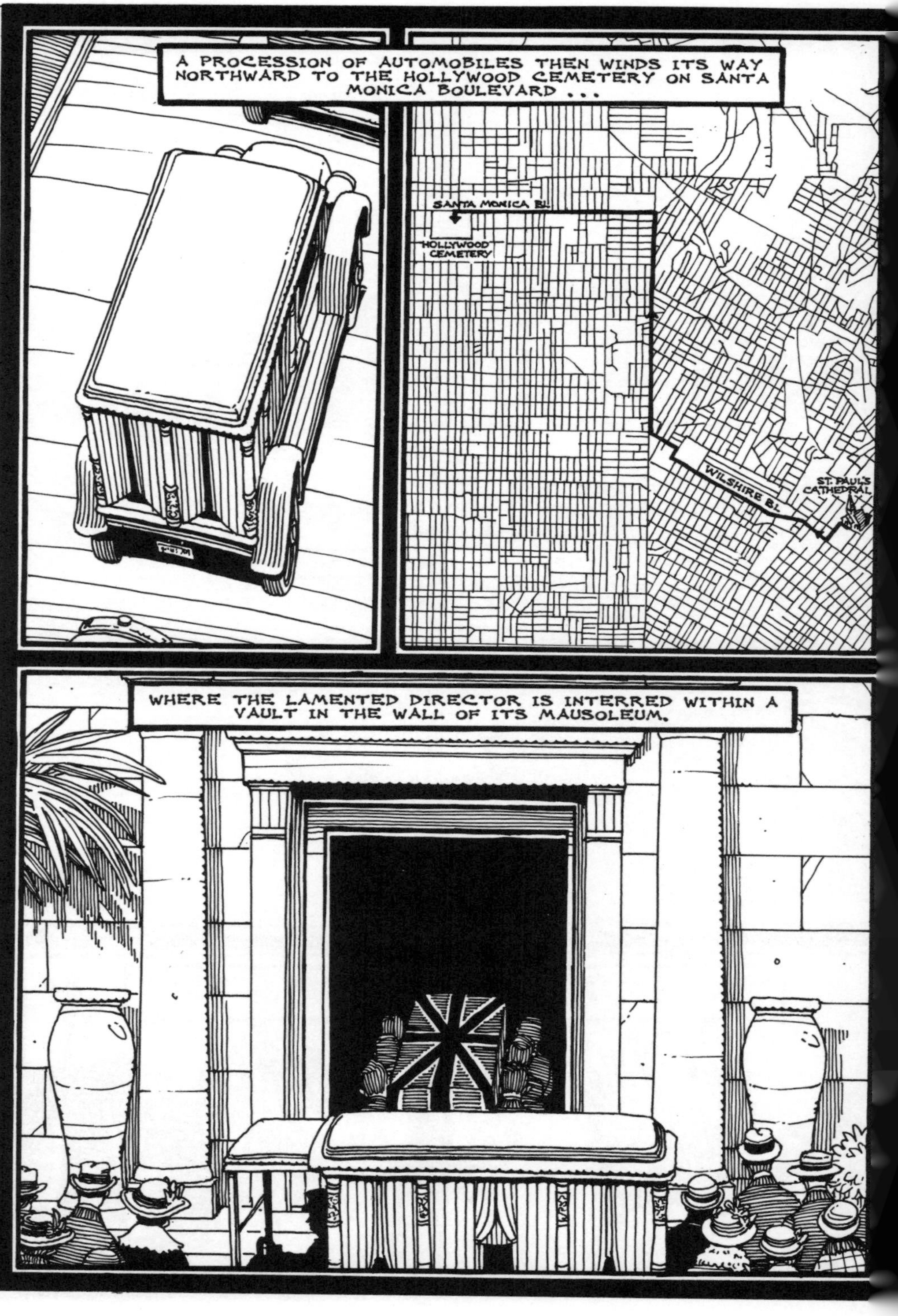
A PROCESSION OF AUTOMOBILES THEN WINDS ITS WAY NORTHWARD TO THE HOLLYWOOD CEMETERY ON SANTA MONICA BOULEVARD ...
SANTA MONICA BL.
HOLLYWOOD CEMETERY
WILSHIRE BL.
ST. PAUL'S CATHEDRAL
WHERE THE LAMENTED DIRECTOR IS INTERRED WITHIN A VAULT IN THE WALL OF ITS MAUSOLEUM.

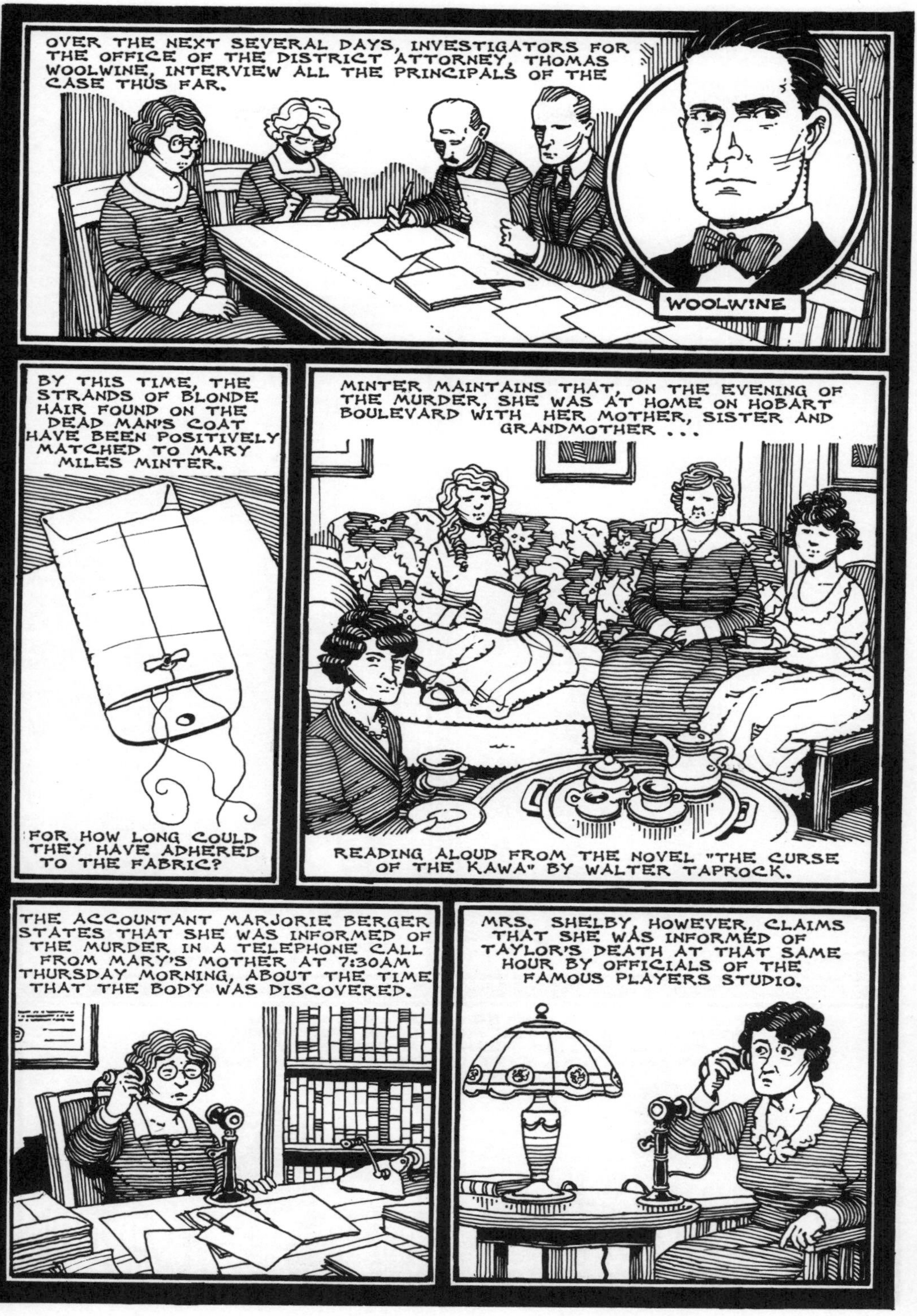
OVER THE NEXT SEVERAL DAYS, INVESTIGATORS FOR THE OFFICE OF THE DISTRICT ATTORNEY, THOMAS WOOLWINE, INTERVIEW ALL THE PRINCIPALS OF THE CASE THUS FAR.
WOOLWINE
BY THIS TIME, THE STRANDS OF BLONDE HAIR FOUND ON THE DEAD MAN'S COAT HAVE BEEN POSITIVELY MATCHED TO MARY MILES MINTER.
FOR HOW LONG COULD THEY HAVE ADHERED TO THE FABRIC?
MINTER MAINTAINS THAT, ON THE EVENING OF THE MURDER, SHE WAS AT HOME ON HOBART BOULEVARD WITH HER MOTHER, SISTER AND GRANDMOTHER ...
READING ALOUD FROM THE NOVEL "THE CURSE OF THE KAWA" BY WALTER TAPROCK.
THE ACCOUNTANT MARJORIE BERGER STATES THAT SHE WAS INFORMED OF THE MURDER IN A TELEPHONE CALL FROM MARY'S MOTHER AT 7:30AM THURSDAY MORNING, ABOUT THE TIME THAT THE BODY WAS DISCOVERED.
MRS. SHELBY, HOWEVER, CLAIMS THAT SHE WAS INFORMED OF TAYLOR'S DEATH AT THAT SAME HOUR BY OFFICIALS OF THE FAMOUS PLAYERS STUDIO.

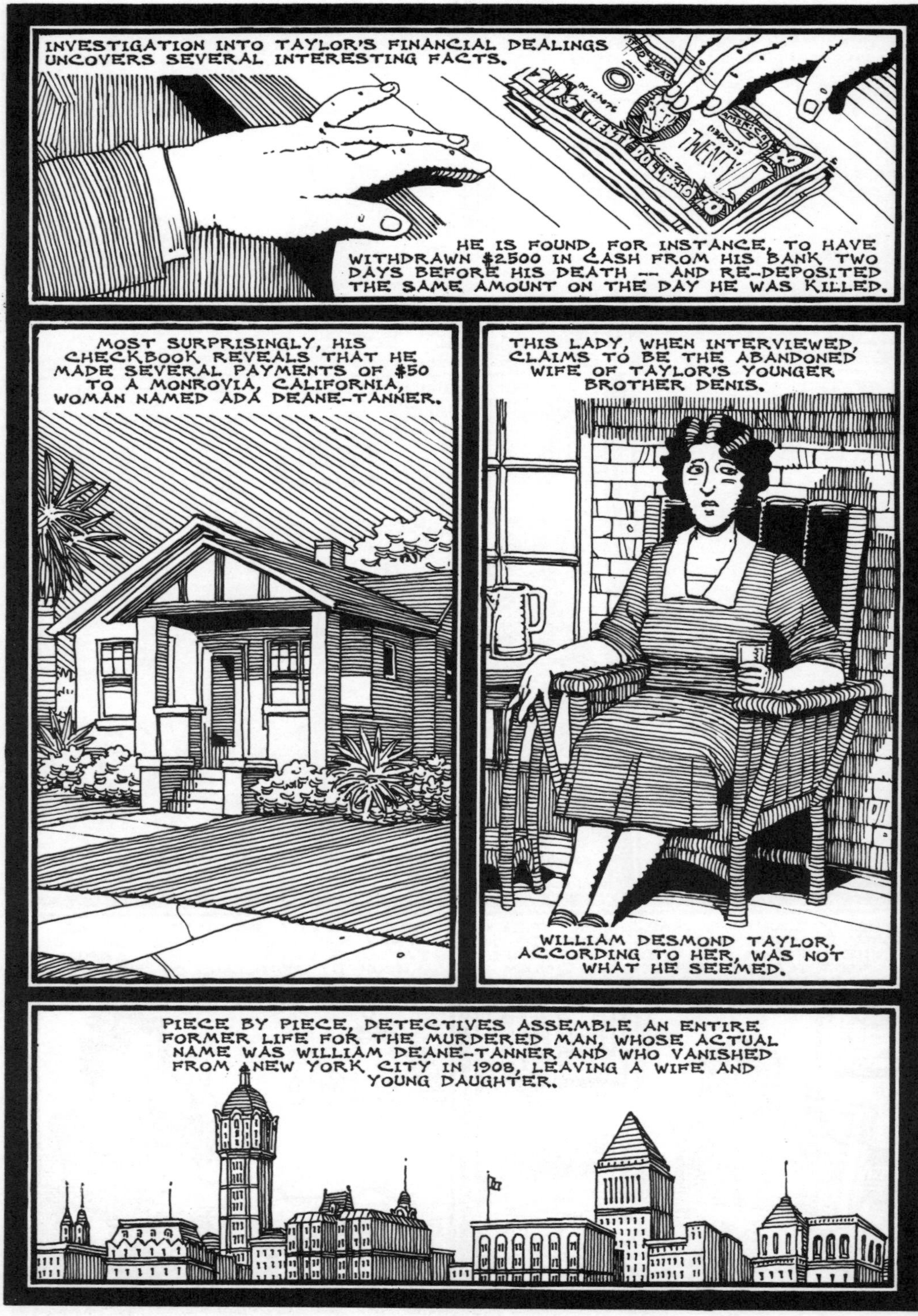
INVESTIGATION INTO TAYLOR'S FINANCIAL DEALINGS UNCOVERS SEVERAL INTERESTING FACTS.
HE IS FOUND, FOR INSTANCE, TO HAVE WITHDRAWN $2500 IN CASH FROM HIS BANK TWO DAYS BEFORE HIS DEATH -- AND RE-DEPOSITED THE SAME AMOUNT ON THE DAY HE WAS KILLED.
MOST SURPRISINGLY, HIS CHECKBOOK REVEALS THAT HE MADE SEVERAL PAYMENTS OF $50 TO A MONROVIA, CALIFORNIA, WOMAN NAMED ADA DEANE-TANNER.
THIS LADY, WHEN INTERVIEWED, CLAIMS TO BE THE ABANDONED WIFE OF TAYLOR'S YOUNGER BROTHER DENIS.
WILLIAM DESMOND TAYLOR, ACCORDING TO HER, WAS NOT WHAT HE SEEMED.
PIECE BY PIECE, DETECTIVES ASSEMBLE AN ENTIRE FORMER LIFE FOR THE MURDERED MAN, WHOSE ACTUAL NAME WAS WILLIAM DEANE-TANNER AND WHO VANISHED FROM NEW YORK CITY IN 1908, LEAVING A WIFE AND YOUNG DAUGHTER.

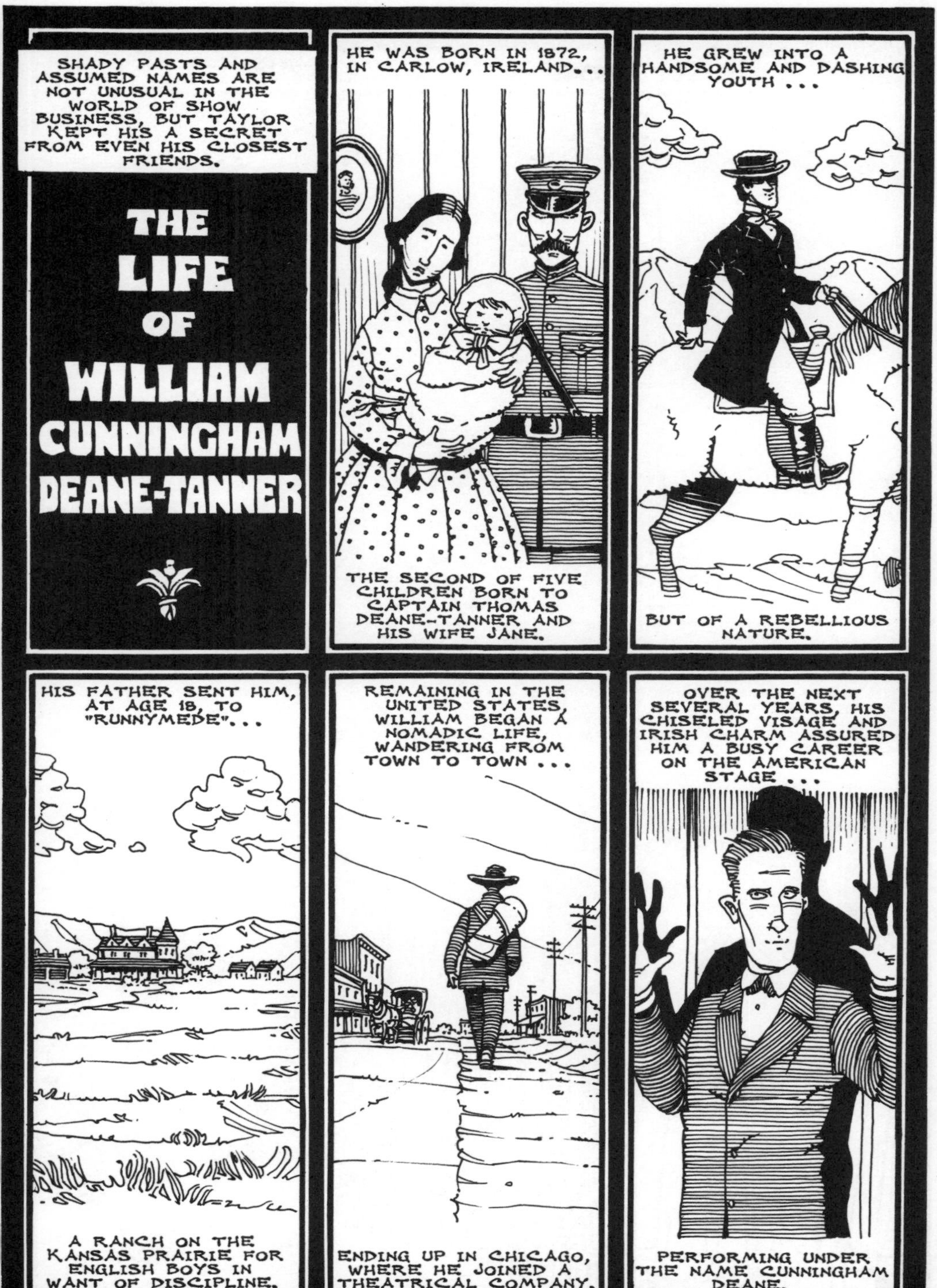
SHADY PASTS AND ASSUMED NAMES ARE NOT UNUSUAL IN THE WORLD OF SHOW BUSINESS, BUT TAYLOR KEPT HIS A SECRET FROM EVEN HIS CLOSEST FRIENDS.
THE LIFE OF WILLIAM CUNNINGHAM DEANE-TANNER
HE WAS BORN IN 1872, IN CARLOW, IRELAND...
THE SECOND OF FIVE CHILDREN BORN TO CAPTAIN THOMAS DEANE-TANNER AND HIS WIFE JANE.
HE GREW INTO A HANDSOME AND DASHING YOUTH ...
BUT OF A REBELLIOUS NATURE.
HIS FATHER SENT HIM, AT AGE 18, TO "RUNNYMEDE"...
A RANCH ON THE KANSAS PRAIRIE FOR ENGLISH BOYS IN WANT OF DISCIPLINE.
REMAINING IN THE UNITED STATES, WILLIAM BEGAN A NOMADIC LIFE, WANDERING FROM TOWN TO TOWN ...
ENDING UP IN CHICAGO, WHERE HE JOINED A THEATRICAL COMPANY.
OVER THE NEXT SEVERAL YEARS, HIS CHISELED VISAGE AND IRISH CHARM ASSURED HIM A BUSY CAREER ON THE AMERICAN STAGE ...
PERFORMING UNDER THE NAME CUNNINGHAM DEANE.

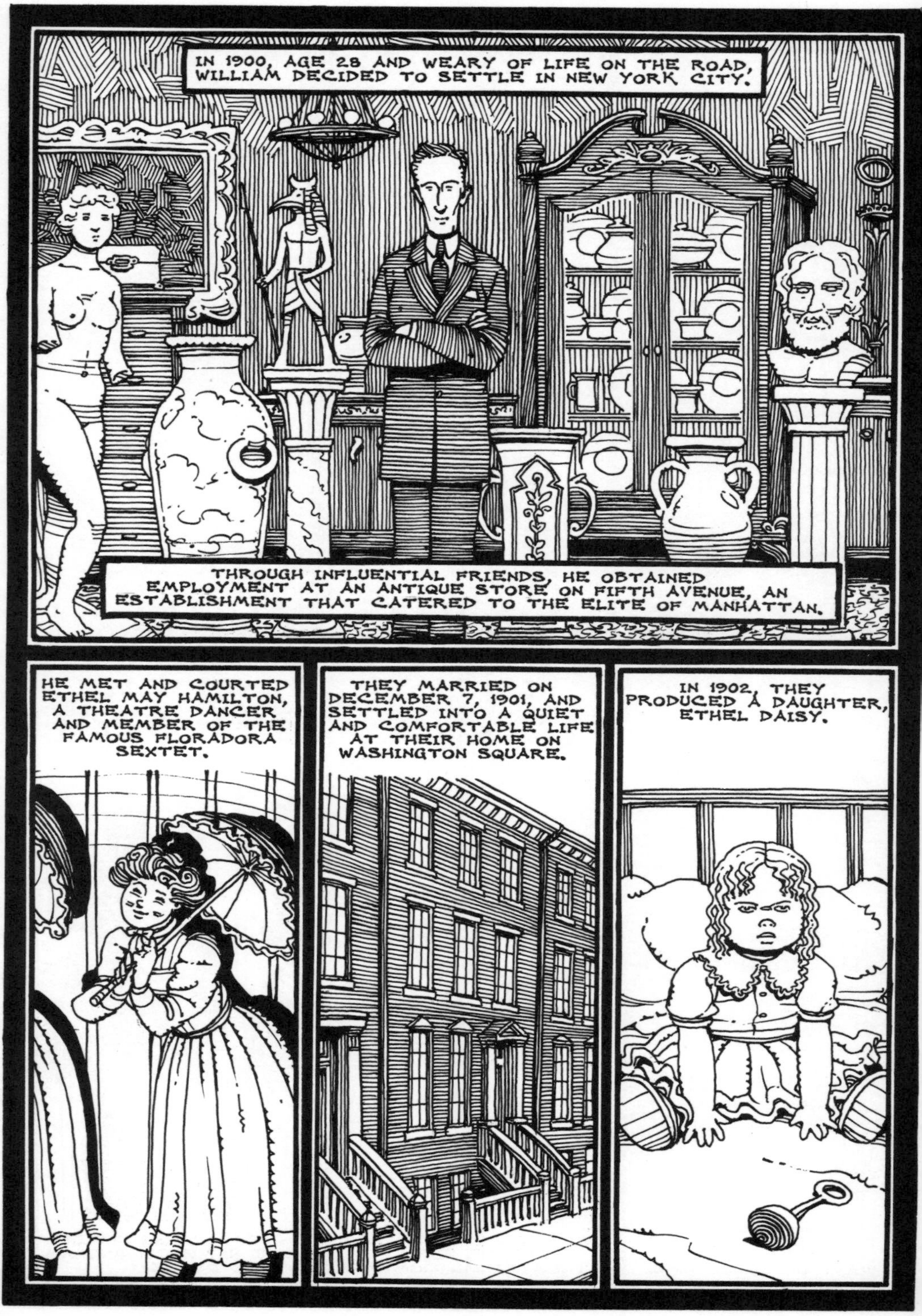
IN 1900, AGE 28 AND WEARY OF LIFE ON THE ROAD, WILLIAM DECIDED TO SETTLE IN NEW YORK CITY.
THROUGH INFLUENTIAL FRIENDS, HE OBTAINED EMPLOYMENT AT AN ANTIQUE STORE ON FIFTH AVENUE, AN ESTABLISHMENT THAT CATERED TO THE ELITE OF MANHATTAN.
HE MET AND COURTED ETHEL MAY HAMILTON, A THEATRE DANCER AND MEMBER OF THE FAMOUS FLORADORA SEXTET.
THEY MARRIED ON DECEMBER 7, 1901, AND SETTLED INTO A QUIET AND COMFORTABLE LIFE AT THEIR HOME ON WASHINGTON SQUARE.
IN 1902, THEY PRODUCED A DAUGHTER, ETHEL DAISY.

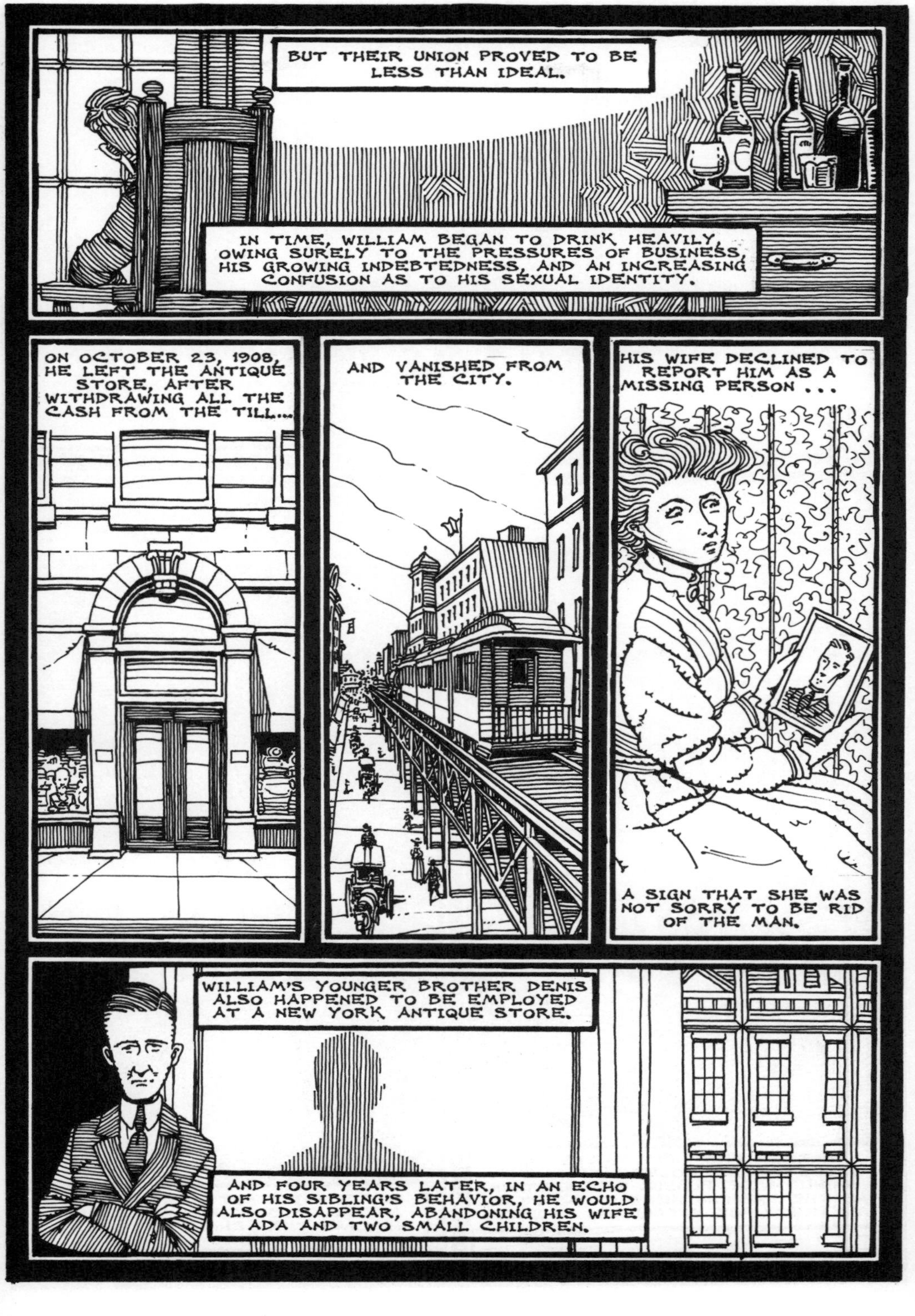
BUT THEIR UNION PROVED TO BE LESS THAN IDEAL.
IN TIME, WILLIAM BEGAN TO DRINK HEAVILY, OWING SURELY TO THE PRESSURES OF BUSINESS, HIS GROWING INDEBTEDNESS, AND AN INCREASING CONFUSION AS TO HIS SEXUAL IDENTITY.
ON OCTOBER 23, 1908, HE LEFT THE ANTIQUE STORE, AFTER WITHDRAWING ALL THE CASH FROM THE TILL...
AND VANISHED FROM THE CITY.
HIS WIFE DECLINED TO REPORT HIM AS A MISSING PERSON . . .
A SIGN THAT SHE WAS NOT SORRY TO BE RID OF THE MAN.
WILLIAM'S YOUNGER BROTHER DENIS ALSO HAPPENED TO BE EMPLOYED AT A NEW YORK ANTIQUE STORE.
AND FOUR YEARS LATER, IN AN ECHO OF HIS SIBLING'S BEHAVIOR, HE WOULD ALSO DISAPPEAR, ABANDONING HIS WIFE ADA AND TWO SMALL CHILDREN.

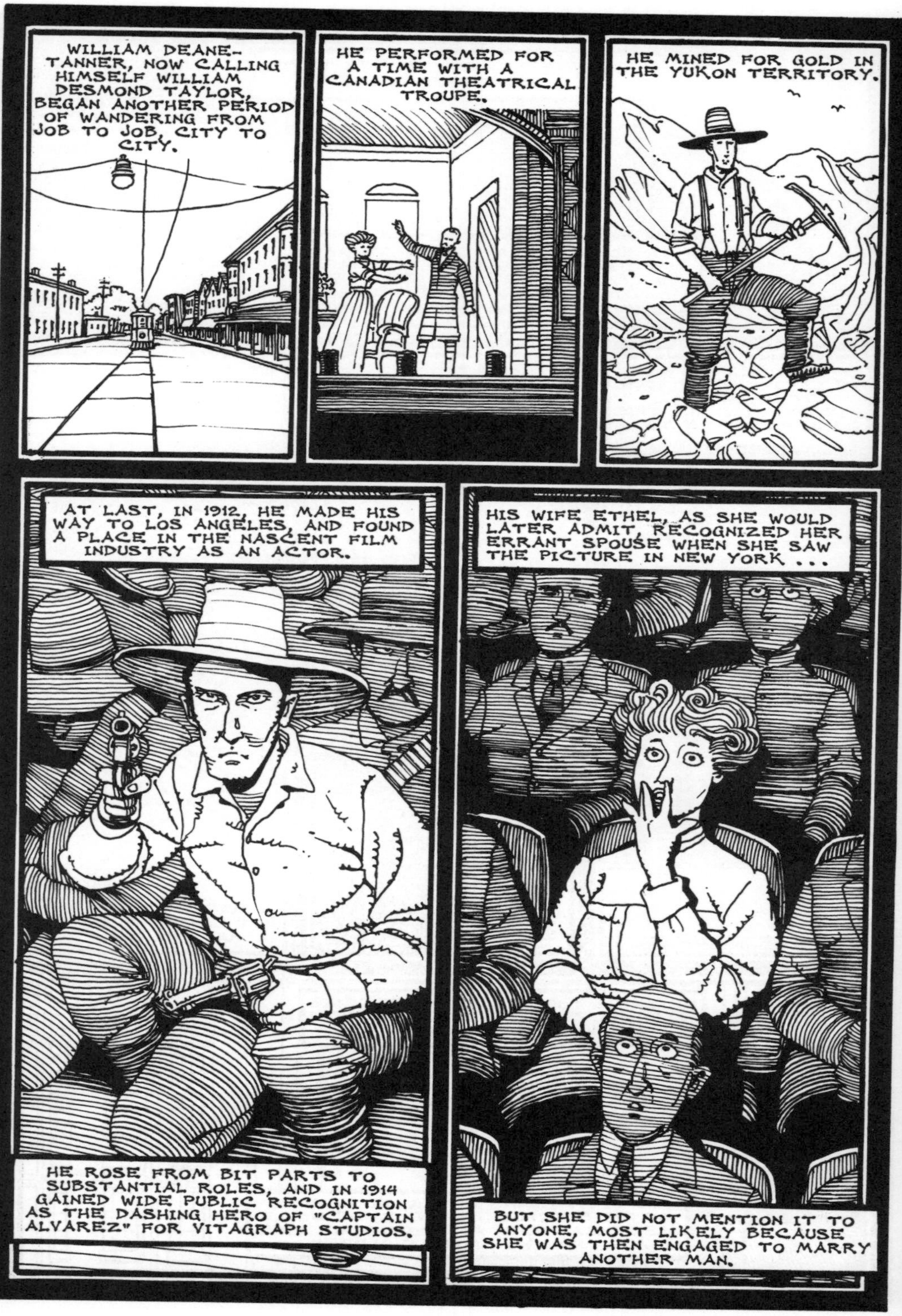
WILLIAM DEANE-TANNER, NOW CALLING HIMSELF WILLIAM DESMOND TAYLOR, BEGAN ANOTHER PERIOD OF WANDERING FROM JOB TO JOB, CITY TO CITY.
HE PERFORMED FOR A TIME WITH A CANADIAN THEATRICAL TROUPE.
HE MINED FOR GOLD IN THE YUKON TERRITORY.
AT LAST, IN 1912, HE MADE HIS WAY TO LOS ANGELES, AND FOUND A PLACE IN THE NASCENT FILM INDUSTRY AS AN ACTOR.
HE ROSE FROM BIT PARTS TO SUBSTANTIAL ROLES, AND IN 1914 GAINED WIDE PUBLIC RECOGNITION AS THE DASHING HERO OF "CAPTAIN ALVAREZ" FOR VITAGRAPH STUDIOS.
HIS WIFE ETHEL, AS SHE WOULD LATER ADMIT, RECOGNIZED HER ERRANT SPOUSE WHEN SHE SAW THE PICTURE IN NEW YORK ...
BUT SHE DID NOT MENTION IT TO ANYONE, MOST LIKELY BECAUSE SHE WAS THEN ENGAGED TO MARRY ANOTHER MAN.

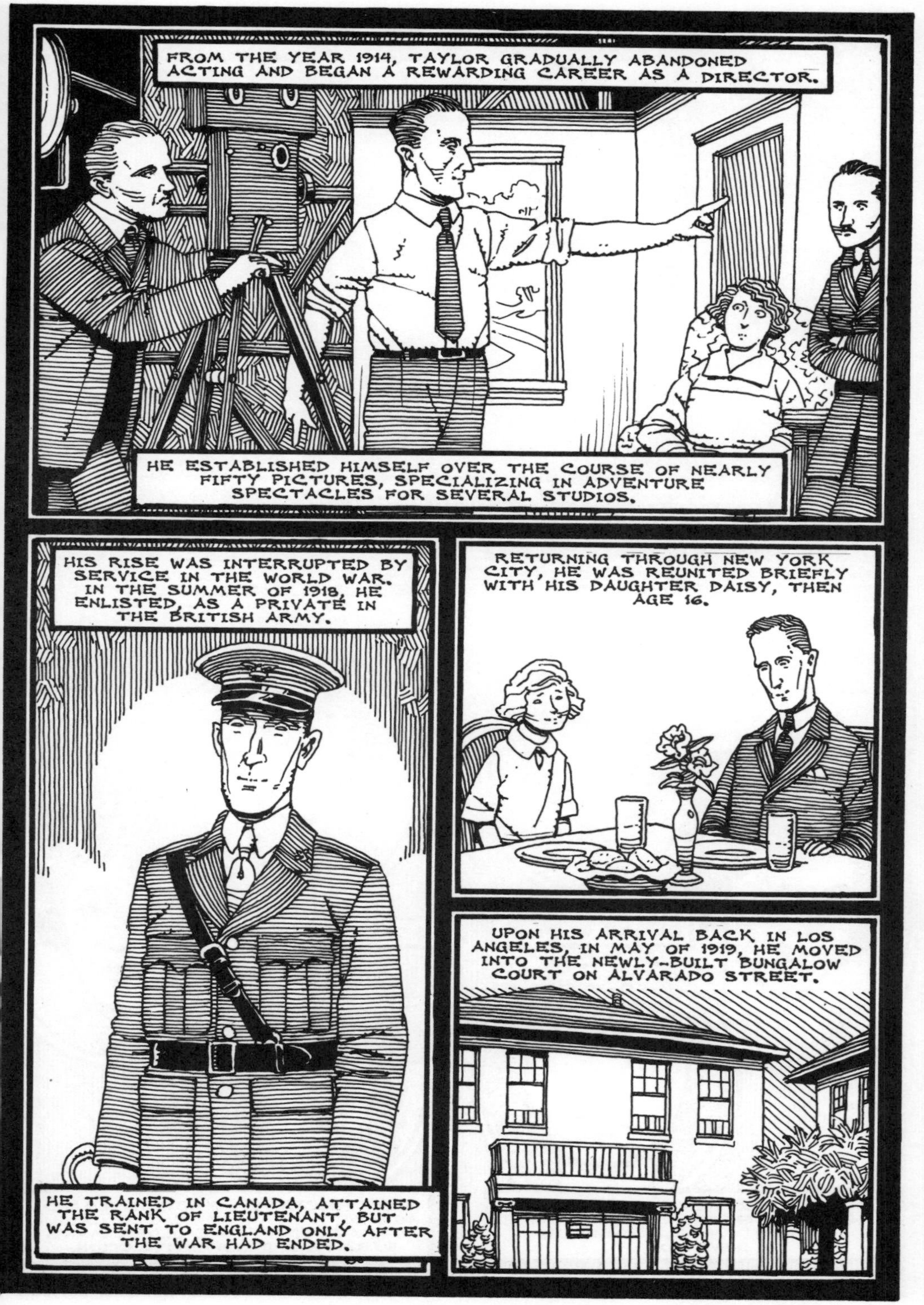
FROM THE YEAR 1914, TAYLOR GRADUALLY ABANDONED ACTING AND BEGAN A REWARDING CAREER AS A DIRECTOR.
HE ESTABLISHED HIMSELF OVER THE COURSE OF NEARLY FIFTY PICTURES, SPECIALIZING IN ADVENTURE SPECTACLES FOR SEVERAL STUDIOS.
HIS RISE WAS INTERRUPTED BY SERVICE IN THE WORLD WAR. IN THE SUMMER OF 1918, HE ENLISTED, AS A PRIVATE IN THE BRITISH ARMY.
HE TRAINED IN CANADA, ATTAINED THE RANK OF LIEUTENANT, BUT WAS SENT TO ENGLAND ONLY AFTER THE WAR HAD ENDED.
RETURNING THROUGH NEW YORK CITY, HE WAS REUNITED BRIEFLY WITH HIS DAUGHTER DAISY, THEN AGE 16.
UPON HIS ARRIVAL BACK IN LOS ANGELES, IN MAY OF 1919, HE MOVED INTO THE NEWLY-BUILT BUNGALOW COURT ON ALVARADO STREET.

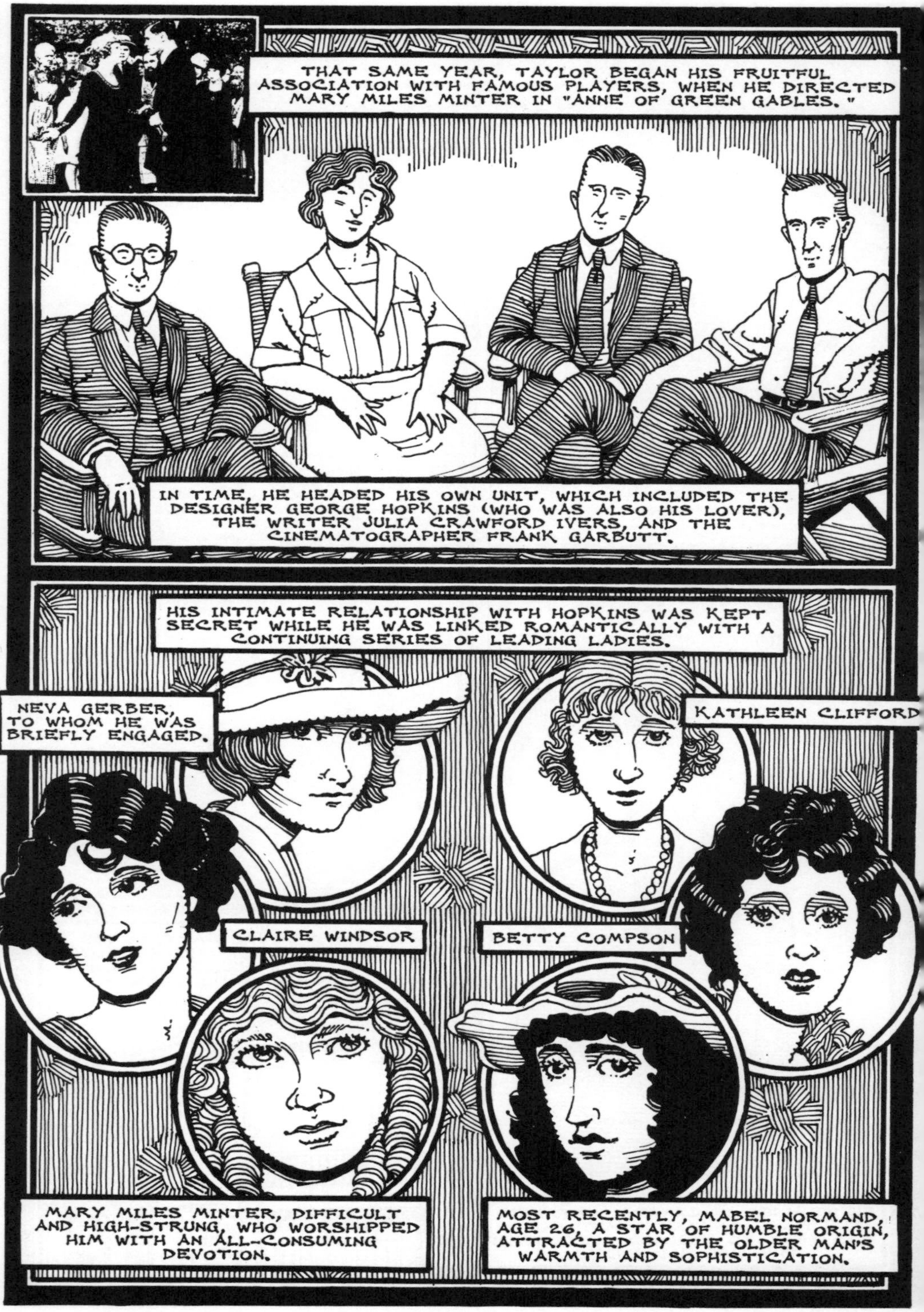
THAT SAME YEAR, TAYLOR BEGAN HIS FRUITFUL ASSOCIATION WITH FAMOUS PLAYERS, WHEN HE DIRECTED MARY MILES MINTER IN "ANNE OF GREEN GABLES."
IN TIME, HE HEADED HIS OWN UNIT, WHICH INCLUDED THE DESIGNER GEORGE HOPKINS (WHO WAS ALSO HIS LOVER), THE WRITER JULIA CRAWFORD IVERS, AND THE CINEMATOGRAPHER FRANK GARBUTT.
HIS INTIMATE RELATIONSHIP WITH HOPKINS WAS KEPT SECRET WHILE HE WAS LINKED ROMANTICALLY WITH A CONTINUING SERIES OF LEADING LADIES.
NEVA GERBER, TO WHOM HE WAS BRIEFLY ENGAGED.
KATHLEEN CLIFFORD
CLAIRE WINDSOR
BETTY COMPSON
MARY MILES MINTER, DIFFICULT AND HIGH-STRUNG, WHO WORSHIPPED HIM WITH AN ALL-CONSUMING DEVOTION.
MOST RECENTLY, MABEL NORMAND, AGE 26, A STAR OF HUMBLE ORIGIN, ATTRACTED BY THE OLDER MAN'S WARMTH AND SOPHISTICATION.

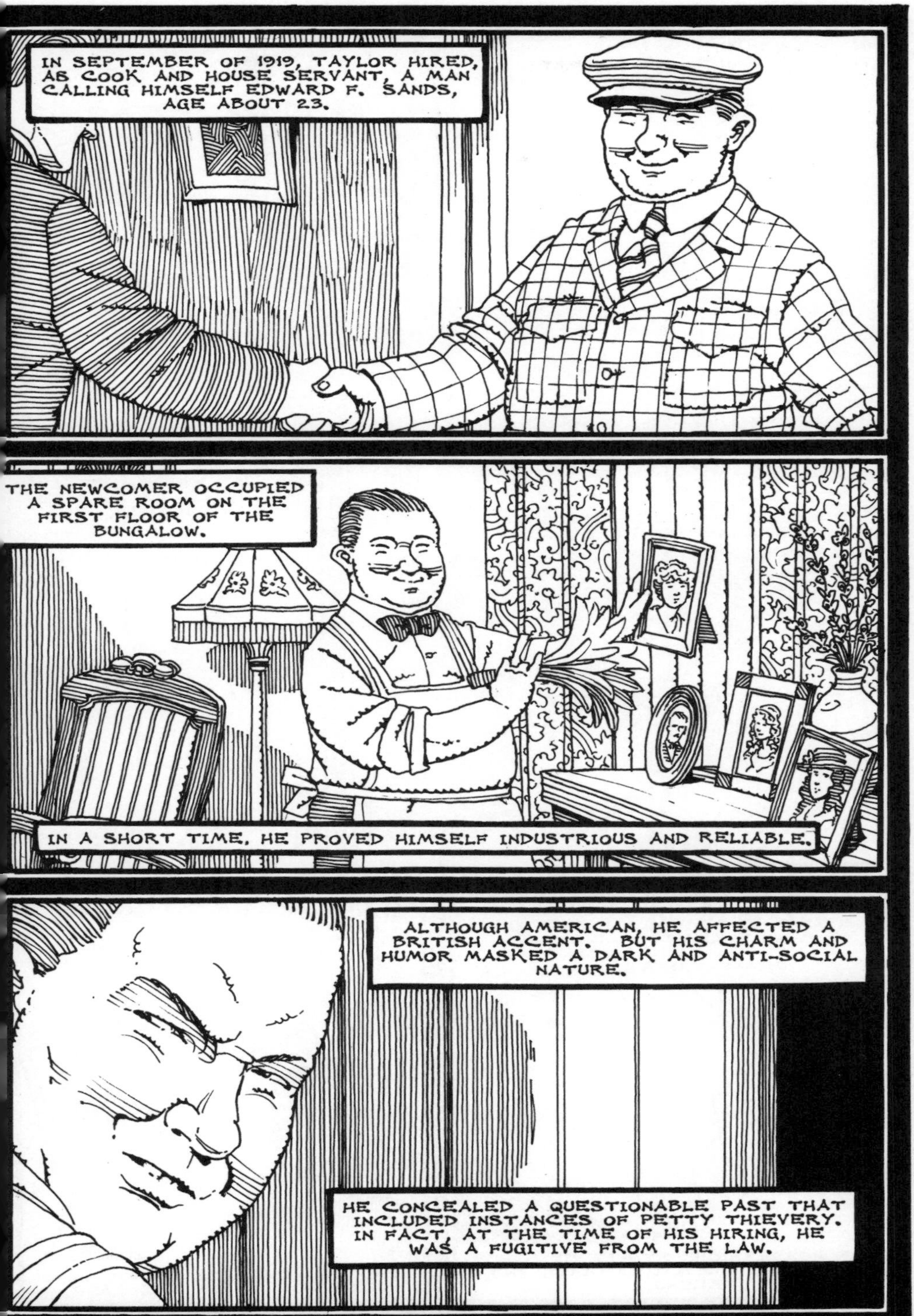
IN SEPTEMBER OF 1919, TAYLOR HIRED, AS COOK AND HOUSE SERVANT, A MAN CALLING HIMSELF EDWARD F. SANDS, AGE ABOUT 23.
THE NEWCOMER OCCUPIED A SPARE ROOM ON THE FIRST FLOOR OF THE BUNGALOW.
IN A SHORT TIME, HE PROVED HIMSELF INDUSTRIOUS AND RELIABLE.
ALTHOUGH AMERICAN, HE AFFECTED A BRITISH ACCENT. BUT HIS CHARM AND HUMOR MASKED A DARK AND ANTI-SOCIAL NATURE.
HE CONCEALED A QUESTIONABLE PAST THAT INCLUDED INSTANCES OF PETTY THIEVERY. IN FACT, AT THE TIME OF HIS HIRING, HE WAS A FUGITIVE FROM THE LAW.

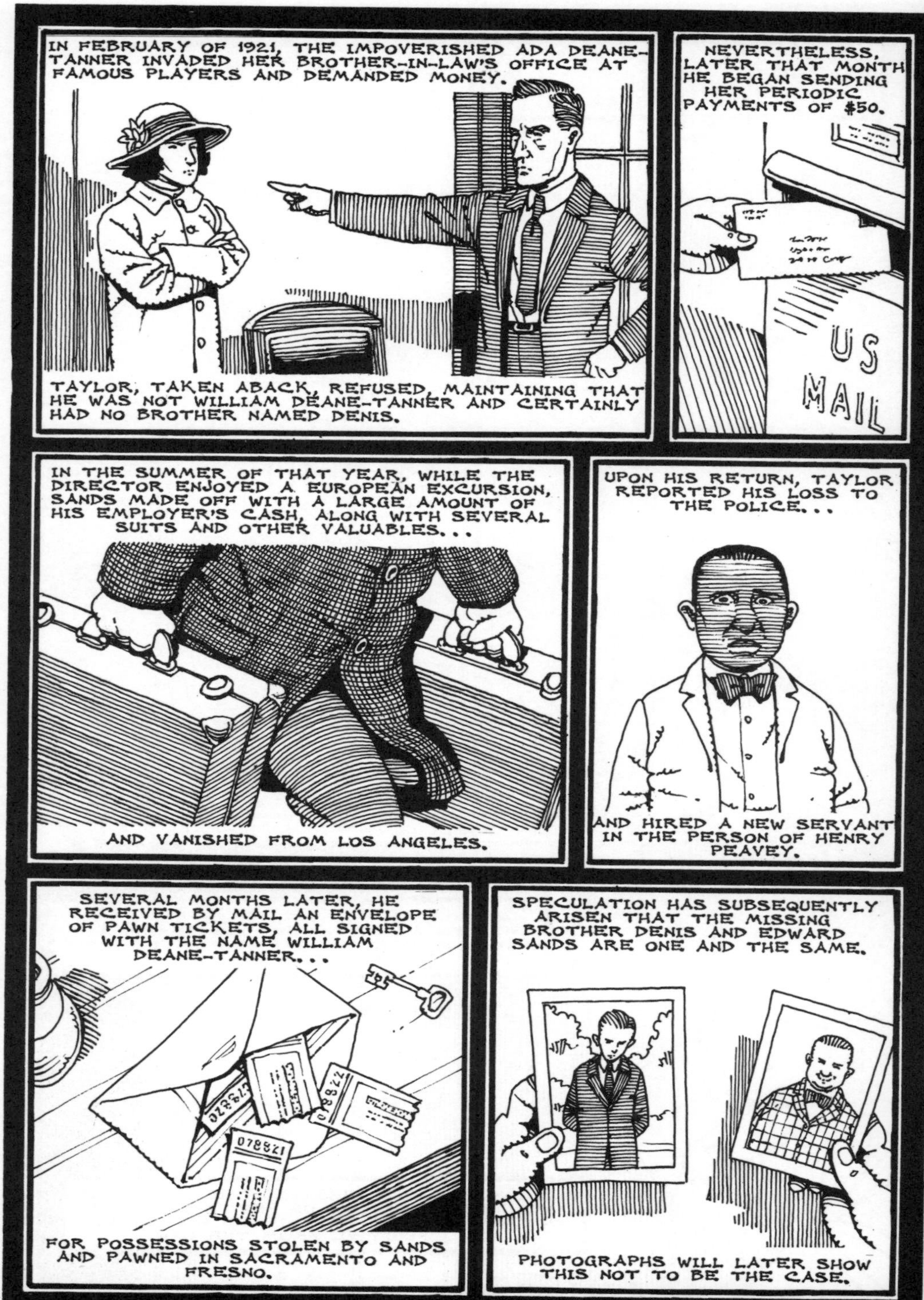

IN FEBRUARY OF 1921, THE IMPOVERISHED ADA DEANE-TANNER INVADED HER BROTHER-IN-LAW'S OFFICE AT FAMOUS PLAYERS AND DEMANDED MONEY.
TAYLOR, TAKEN ABACK, REFUSED, MAINTAINING THAT HE WAS NOT WILLIAM DEANE-TANNER AND CERTAINLY HAD NO BROTHER NAMED DENIS.
NEVERTHELESS, LATER THAT MONTH HE BEGAN SENDING HER PERIODIC PAYMENTS OF $50.
US MAIL
IN THE SUMMER OF THAT YEAR, WHILE THE DIRECTOR ENJOYED A EUROPEAN EXCURSION, SANDS MADE OFF WITH A LARGE AMOUNT OF HIS EMPLOYER'S CASH, ALONG WITH SEVERAL SUITS AND OTHER VALUABLES...
AND VANISHED FROM LOS ANGELES.
UPON HIS RETURN, TAYLOR REPORTED HIS LOSS TO THE POLICE...
AND HIRED A NEW SERVANT IN THE PERSON OF HENRY PEAVEY.
SEVERAL MONTHS LATER, HE RECEIVED BY MAIL AN ENVELOPE OF PAWN TICKETS, ALL SIGNED WITH THE NAME WILLIAM DEANE-TANNER...
FOR POSSESSIONS STOLEN BY SANDS AND PAWNED IN SACRAMENTO AND FRESNO.
SPECULATION HAS SUBSEQUENTLY ARISEN THAT THE MISSING BROTHER DENIS AND EDWARD SANDS ARE ONE AND THE SAME.
PHOTOGRAPHS WILL LATER SHOW THIS NOT TO BE THE CASE.

PART V

THE SUSPECTS

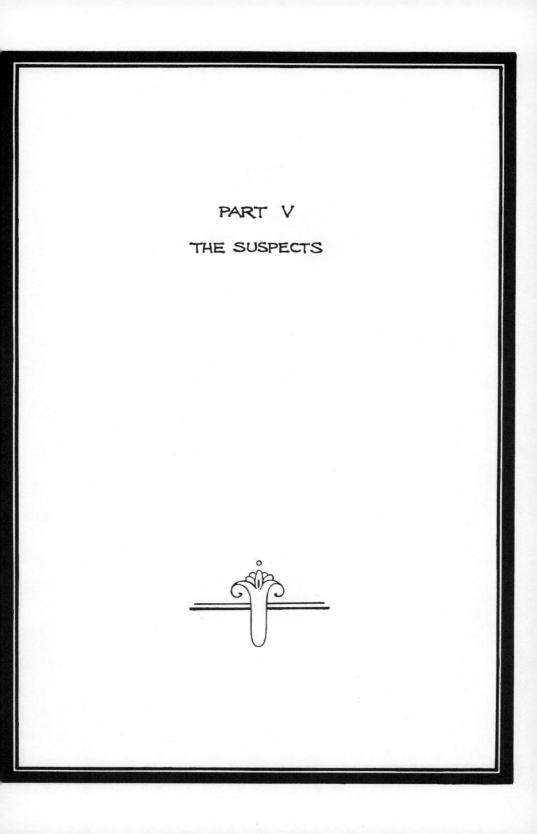

STARS OF THE PHOTOPLAY

FRANCIS X. BUSHMAN

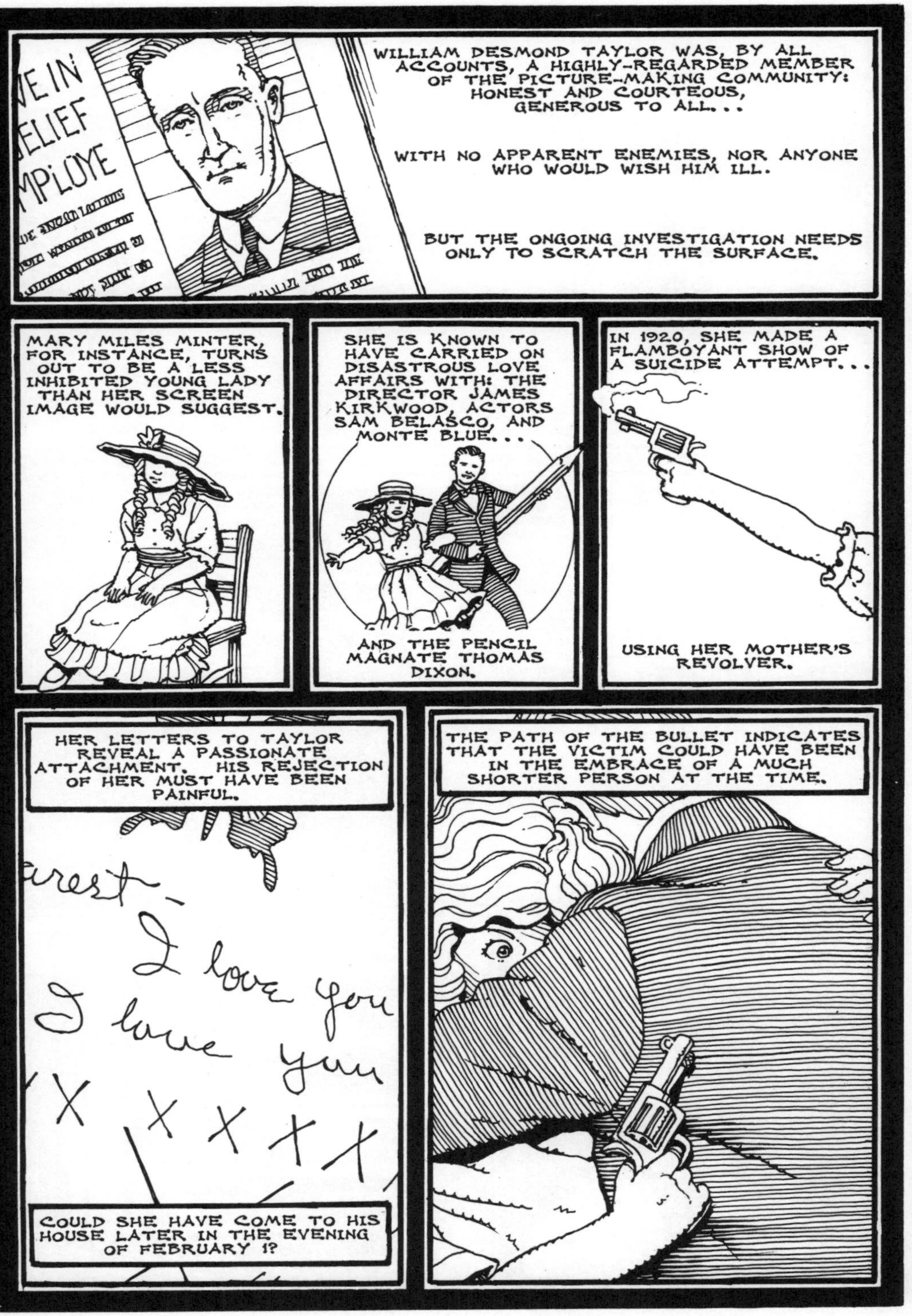

VE IN
BELIEF
MPLOYE
WILLIAM DESMOND TAYLOR WAS, BY ALL ACCOUNTS, A HIGHLY-REGARDED MEMBER OF THE PICTURE-MAKING COMMUNITY: HONEST AND COURTEOUS, GENEROUS TO ALL...
WITH NO APPARENT ENEMIES, NOR ANYONE WHO WOULD WISH HIM ILL.
BUT THE ONGOING INVESTIGATION NEEDS ONLY TO SCRATCH THE SURFACE.
MARY MILES MINTER, FOR INSTANCE, TURNS OUT TO BE A LESS INHIBITED YOUNG LADY THAN HER SCREEN IMAGE WOULD SUGGEST.
SHE IS KNOWN TO HAVE CARRIED ON DISASTROUS LOVE AFFAIRS WITH: THE DIRECTOR JAMES KIRKWOOD, ACTORS SAM BELASCO, AND MONTE BLUE...
AND THE PENCIL MAGNATE THOMAS DIXON.
IN 1920, SHE MADE A FLAMBOYANT SHOW OF A SUICIDE ATTEMPT...
USING HER MOTHER'S REVOLVER.
HER LETTERS TO TAYLOR REVEAL A PASSIONATE ATTACHMENT. HIS REJECTION OF HER MUST HAVE BEEN PAINFUL.
arest -
I love you
I love you
X X X X X X
COULD SHE HAVE COME TO HIS HOUSE LATER IN THE EVENING OF FEBRUARY 1?
THE PATH OF THE BULLET INDICATES THAT THE VICTIM COULD HAVE BEEN IN THE EMBRACE OF A MUCH SHORTER PERSON AT THE TIME.

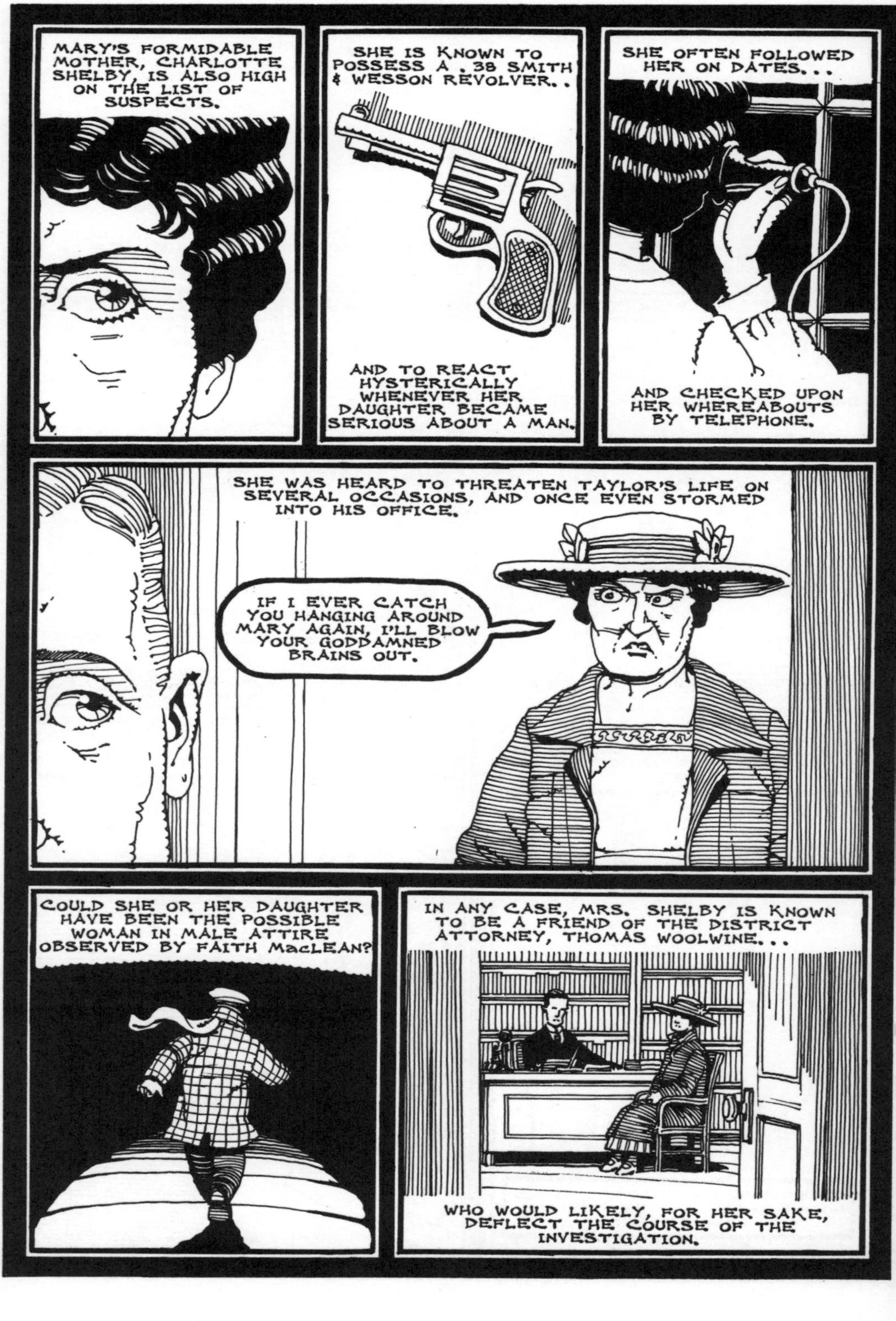
MARY'S FORMIDABLE MOTHER, CHARLOTTE SHELBY, IS ALSO HIGH ON THE LIST OF SUSPECTS.
SHE IS KNOWN TO POSSESS A .38 SMITH & WESSON REVOLVER. .
AND TO REACT HYSTERICALLY WHENEVER HER DAUGHTER BECAME SERIOUS ABOUT A MAN.
SHE OFTEN FOLLOWED HER ON DATES. . .
AND CHECKED UPON HER WHEREABOUTS BY TELEPHONE.
SHE WAS HEARD TO THREATEN TAYLOR'S LIFE ON SEVERAL OCCASIONS, AND ONCE EVEN STORMED INTO HIS OFFICE.
IF I EVER CATCH YOU HANGING AROUND MARY AGAIN, I'LL BLOW YOUR GODDAMNED BRAINS OUT.
COULD SHE OR HER DAUGHTER HAVE BEEN THE POSSIBLE WOMAN IN MALE ATTIRE OBSERVED BY FAITH MacLEAN?
IN ANY CASE, MRS. SHELBY IS KNOWN TO BE A FRIEND OF THE DISTRICT ATTORNEY, THOMAS WOOLWINE. . .
WHO WOULD LIKELY, FOR HER SAKE, DEFLECT THE COURSE OF THE INVESTIGATION.

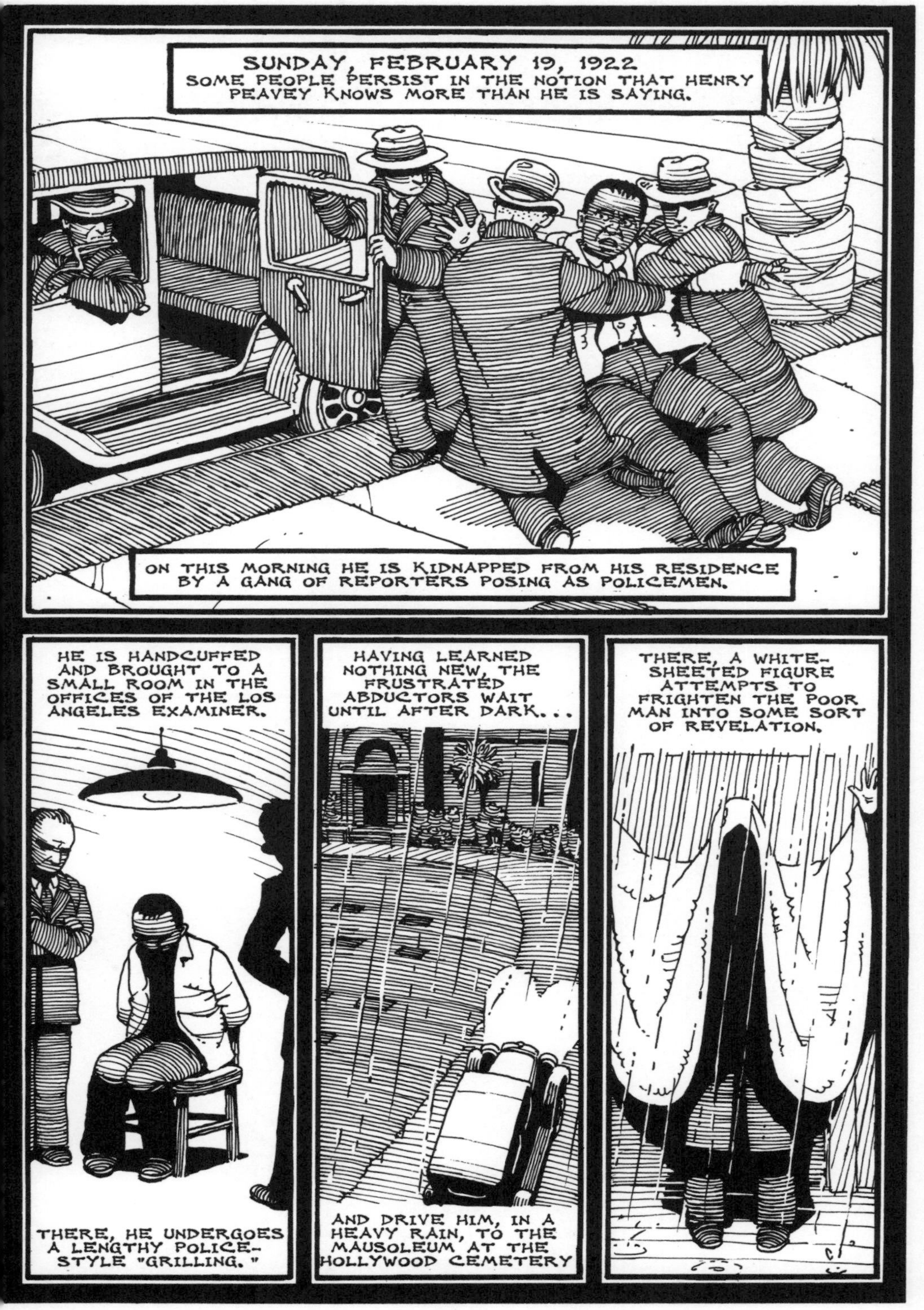
SUNDAY, FEBRUARY 19, 1922
SOME PEOPLE PERSIST IN THE NOTION THAT HENRY PEAVEY KNOWS MORE THAN HE IS SAYING.
ON THIS MORNING HE IS KIDNAPPED FROM HIS RESIDENCE BY A GANG OF REPORTERS POSING AS POLICEMEN.
HE IS HANDCUFFED AND BROUGHT TO A SMALL ROOM IN THE OFFICES OF THE LOS ANGELES EXAMINER.
THERE, HE UNDERGOES A LENGTHY POLICE-STYLE "GRILLING."
HAVING LEARNED NOTHING NEW, THE FRUSTRATED ABDUCTORS WAIT UNTIL AFTER DARK...
AND DRIVE HIM, IN A HEAVY RAIN, TO THE MAUSOLEUM AT THE HOLLYWOOD CEMETERY
THERE, A WHITE-SHEETED FIGURE ATTEMPTS TO FRIGHTEN THE POOR MAN INTO SOME SORT OF REVELATION.

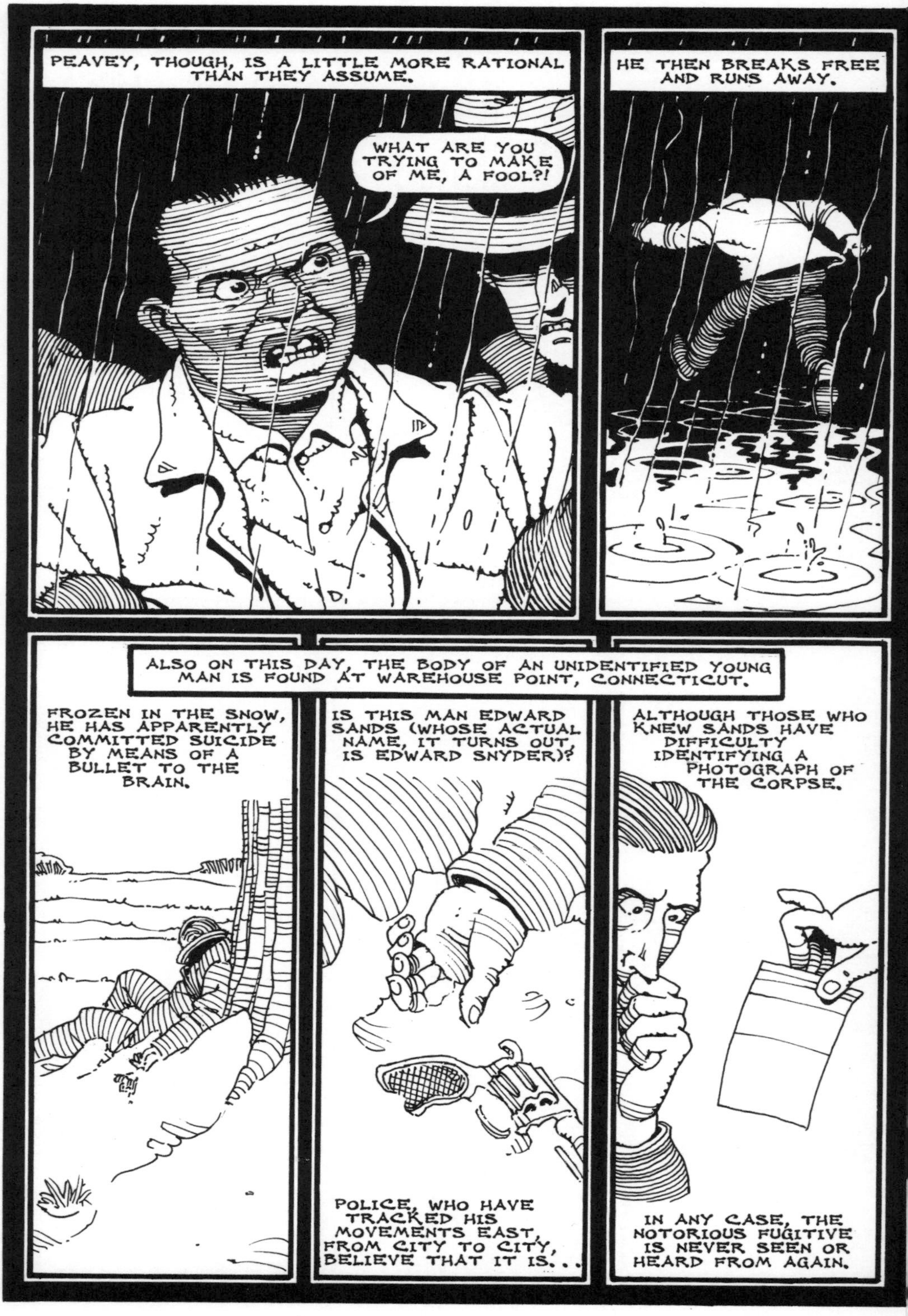
PEAVEY, THOUGH, IS A LITTLE MORE RATIONAL THAN THEY ASSUME.
WHAT ARE YOU TRYING TO MAKE OF ME, A FOOL?!
HE THEN BREAKS FREE AND RUNS AWAY.
ALSO ON THIS DAY, THE BODY OF AN UNIDENTIFIED YOUNG MAN IS FOUND AT WAREHOUSE POINT, CONNECTICUT.
FROZEN IN THE SNOW, HE HAS APPARENTLY COMMITTED SUICIDE BY MEANS OF A BULLET TO THE BRAIN.
IS THIS MAN EDWARD SANDS (WHOSE ACTUAL NAME, IT TURNS OUT, IS EDWARD SNYDER)?
POLICE, WHO HAVE TRACKED HIS MOVEMENTS EAST, FROM CITY TO CITY, BELIEVE THAT IT IS...
ALTHOUGH THOSE WHO KNEW SANDS HAVE DIFFICULTY IDENTIFYING A PHOTOGRAPH OF THE CORPSE.
IN ANY CASE, THE NOTORIOUS FUGITIVE IS NEVER SEEN OR HEARD FROM AGAIN.

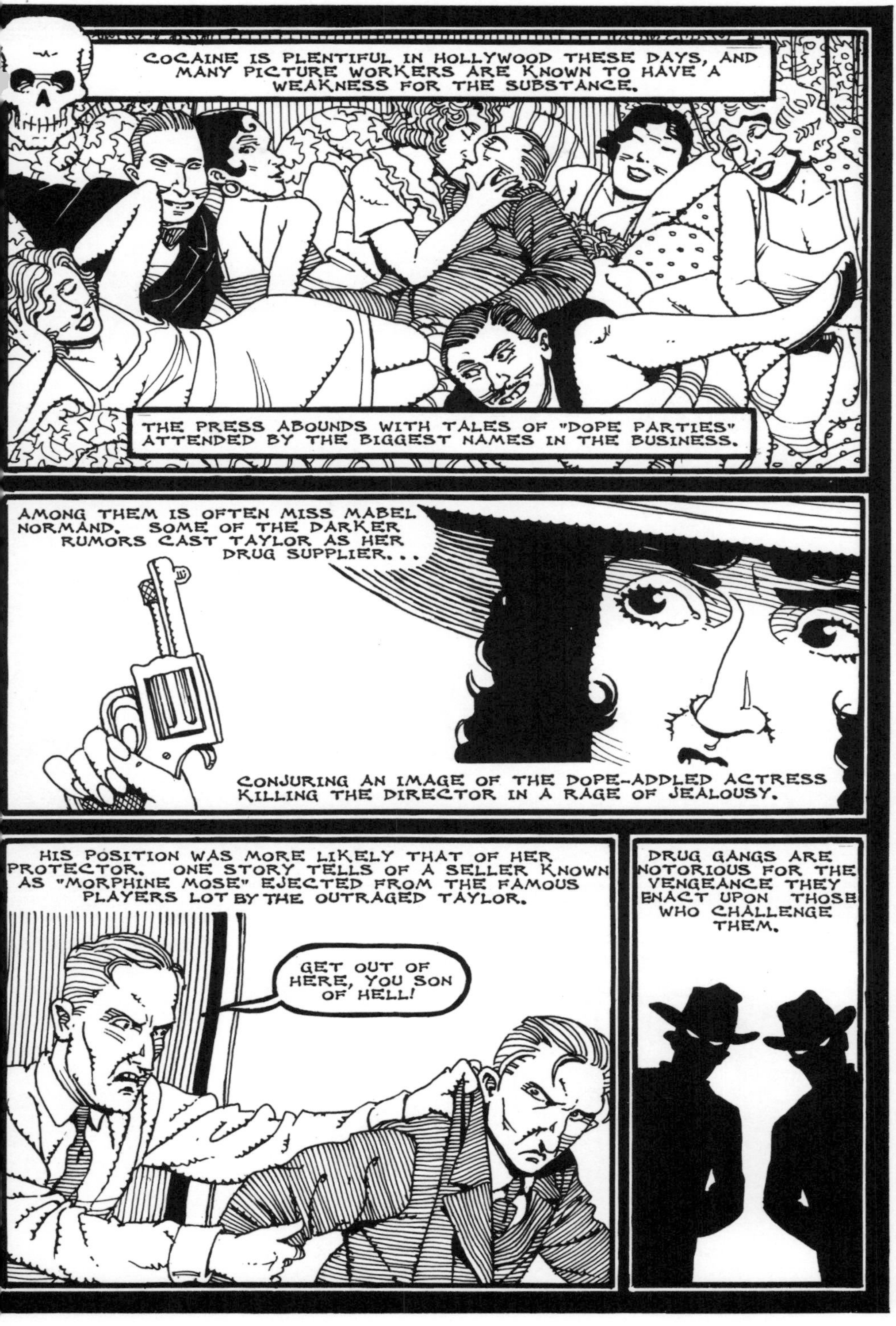
COCAINE IS PLENTIFUL IN HOLLYWOOD THESE DAYS, AND MANY PICTURE WORKERS ARE KNOWN TO HAVE A WEAKNESS FOR THE SUBSTANCE.
THE PRESS ABOUNDS WITH TALES OF "DOPE PARTIES" ATTENDED BY THE BIGGEST NAMES IN THE BUSINESS.
AMONG THEM IS OFTEN MISS MABEL NORMAND. SOME OF THE DARKER RUMORS CAST TAYLOR AS HER DRUG SUPPLIER. . .
CONJURING AN IMAGE OF THE DOPE-ADDLED ACTRESS KILLING THE DIRECTOR IN A RAGE OF JEALOUSY.
HIS POSITION WAS MORE LIKELY THAT OF HER PROTECTOR. ONE STORY TELLS OF A SELLER KNOWN AS "MORPHINE MOSE" EJECTED FROM THE FAMOUS PLAYERS LOT BY THE OUTRAGED TAYLOR.
GET OUT OF HERE, YOU SON OF HELL!
DRUG GANGS ARE NOTORIOUS FOR THE VENGEANCE THEY ENACT UPON THOSE WHO CHALLENGE THEM.

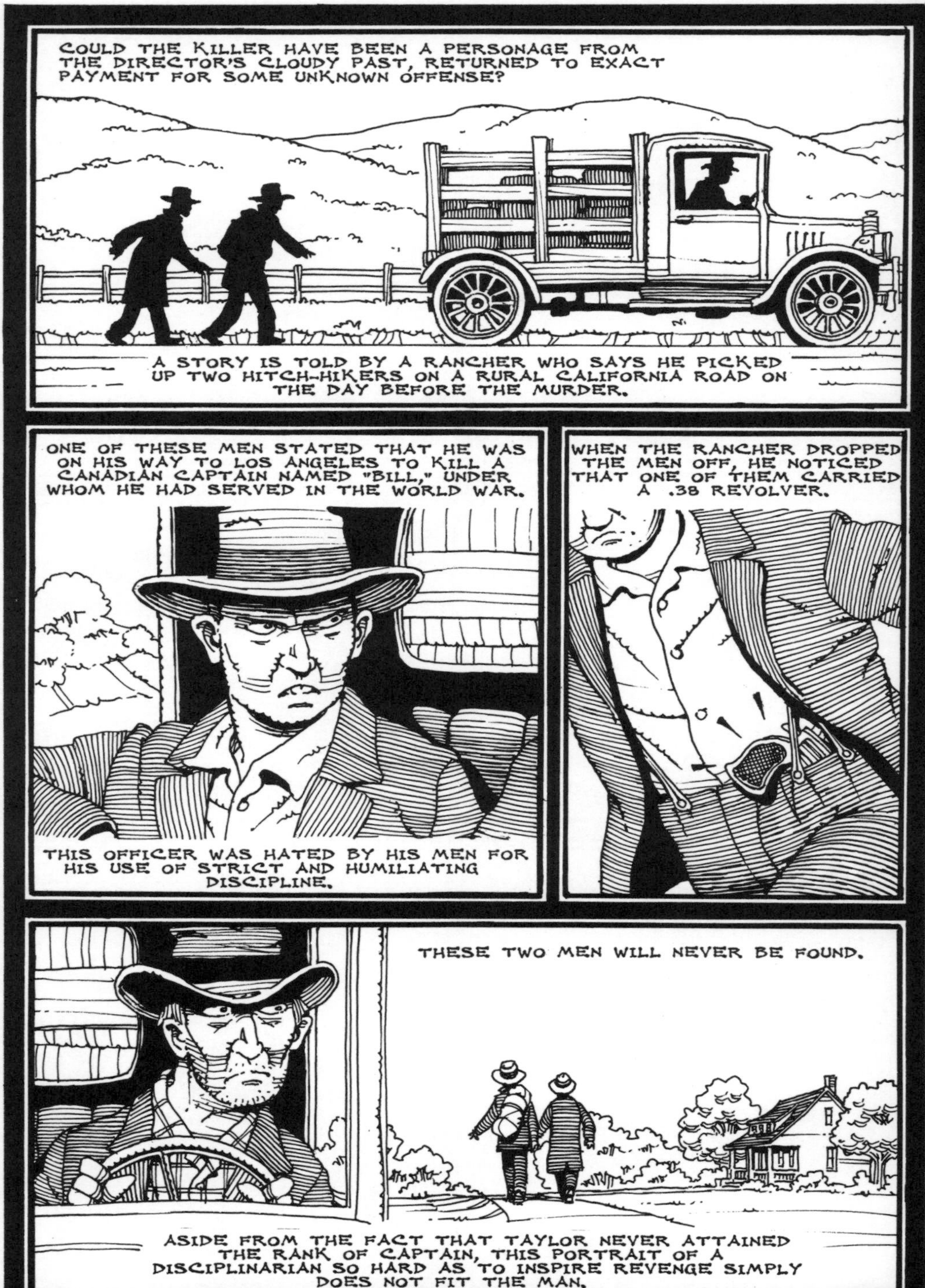
COULD THE KILLER HAVE BEEN A PERSONAGE FROM THE DIRECTOR'S CLOUDY PAST, RETURNED TO EXACT PAYMENT FOR SOME UNKNOWN OFFENSE?
A STORY IS TOLD BY A RANCHER WHO SAYS HE PICKED UP TWO HITCH-HIKERS ON A RURAL CALIFORNIA ROAD ON THE DAY BEFORE THE MURDER.
ONE OF THESE MEN STATED THAT HE WAS ON HIS WAY TO LOS ANGELES TO KILL A CANADIAN CAPTAIN NAMED "BILL," UNDER WHOM HE HAD SERVED IN THE WORLD WAR.
THIS OFFICER WAS HATED BY HIS MEN FOR HIS USE OF STRICT AND HUMILIATING DISCIPLINE.
WHEN THE RANCHER DROPPED THE MEN OFF, HE NOTICED THAT ONE OF THEM CARRIED A .38 REVOLVER.
THESE TWO MEN WILL NEVER BE FOUND.
ASIDE FROM THE FACT THAT TAYLOR NEVER ATTAINED THE RANK OF CAPTAIN, THIS PORTRAIT OF A DISCIPLINARIAN SO HARD AS TO INSPIRE REVENGE SIMPLY DOES NOT FIT THE MAN.

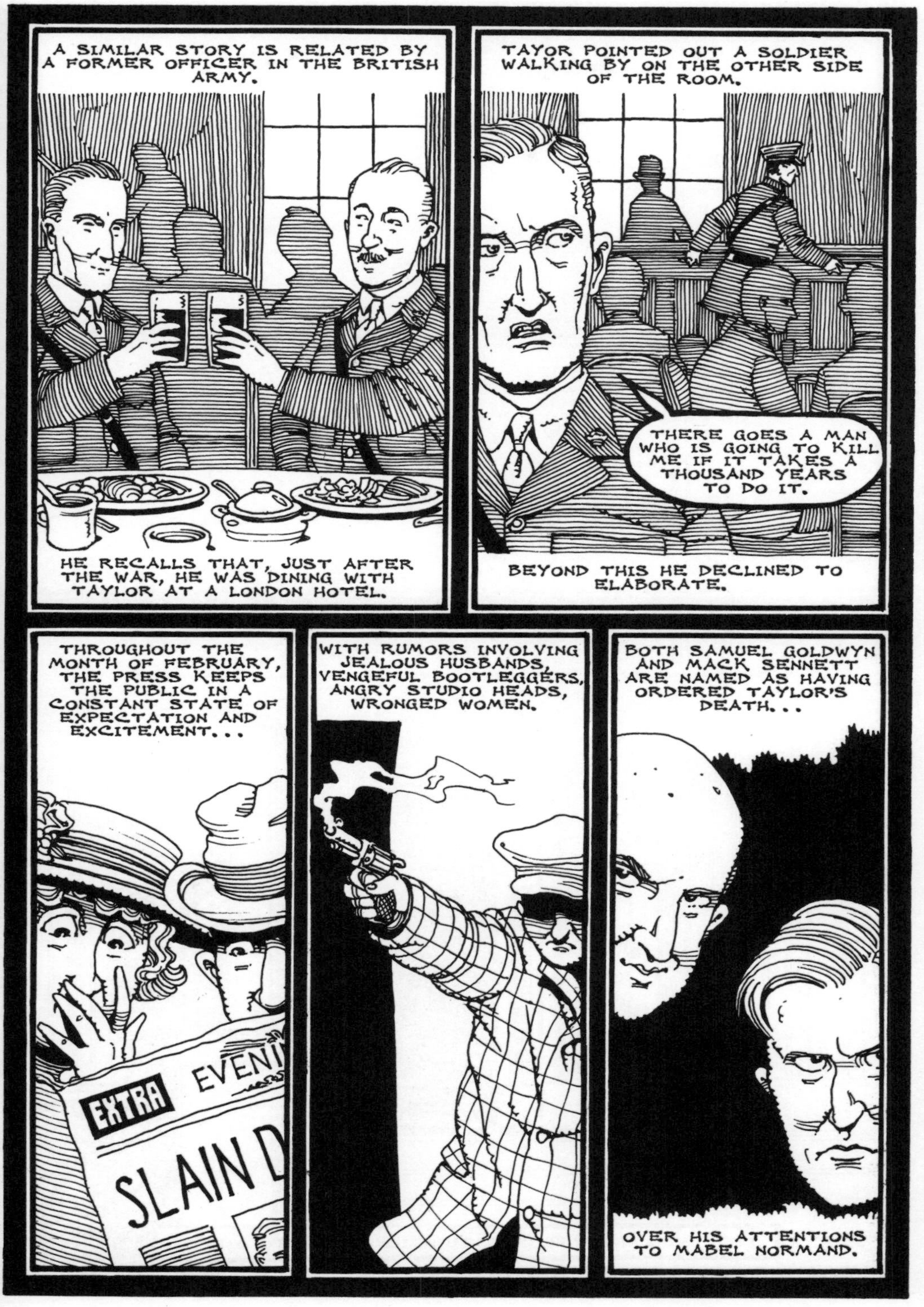
A SIMILAR STORY IS RELATED BY A FORMER OFFICER IN THE BRITISH ARMY.
HE RECALLS THAT, JUST AFTER THE WAR, HE WAS DINING WITH TAYLOR AT A LONDON HOTEL.
TAYOR POINTED OUT A SOLDIER WALKING BY ON THE OTHER SIDE OF THE ROOM.
THERE GOES A MAN WHO IS GOING TO KILL ME IF IT TAKES A THOUSAND YEARS TO DO IT.
BEYOND THIS HE DECLINED TO ELABORATE.
THROUGHOUT THE MONTH OF FEBRUARY, THE PRESS KEEPS THE PUBLIC IN A CONSTANT STATE OF EXPECTATION AND EXCITEMENT...
EXTRA
EVENI
SLAIN D
WITH RUMORS INVOLVING JEALOUS HUSBANDS, VENGEFUL BOOTLEGGERS, ANGRY STUDIO HEADS, WRONGED WOMEN.
BOTH SAMUEL GOLDWYN AND MACK SENNETT ARE NAMED AS HAVING ORDERED TAYLOR'S DEATH...
OVER HIS ATTENTIONS TO MABEL NORMAND.

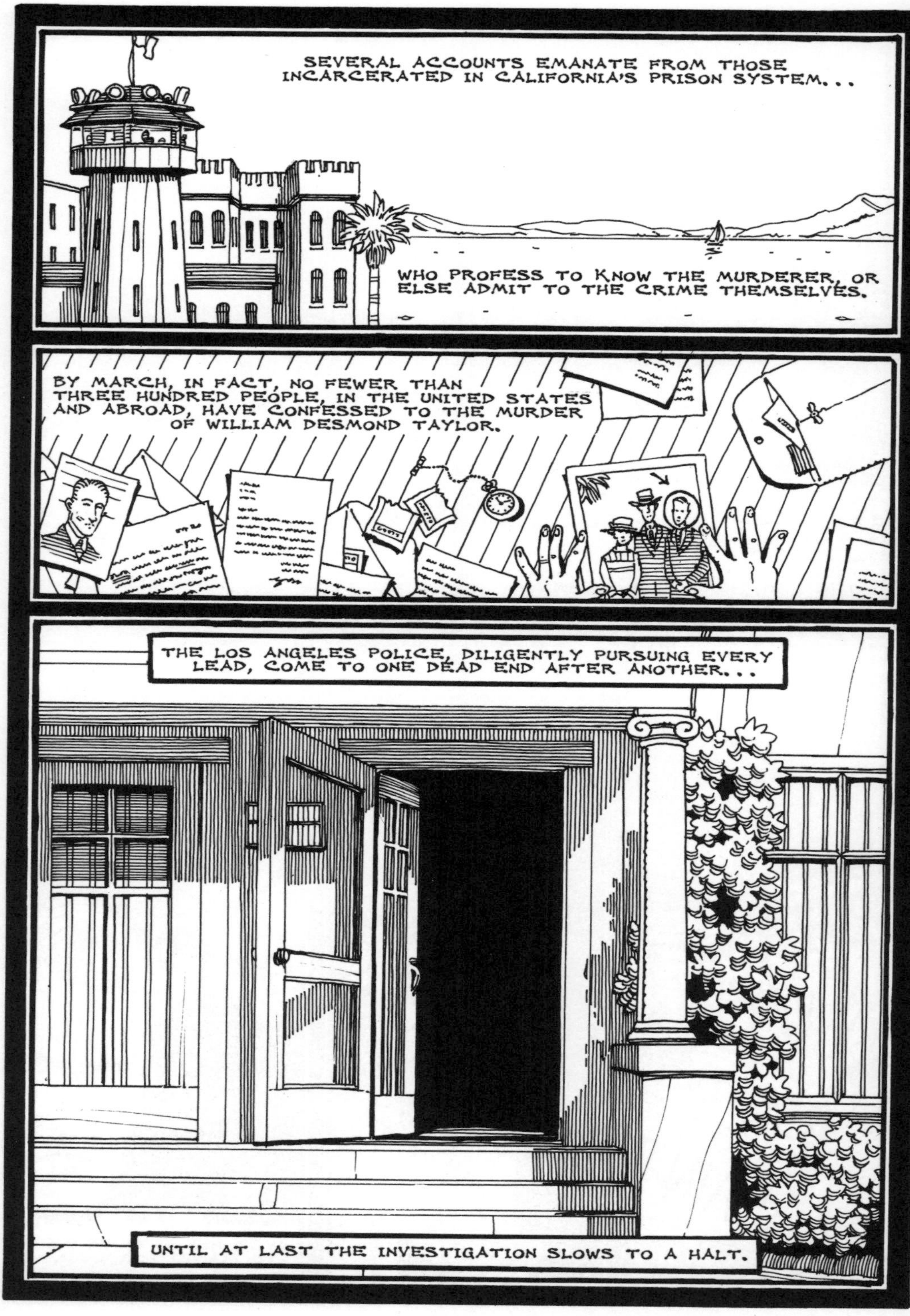
SEVERAL ACCOUNTS EMANATE FROM THOSE INCARCERATED IN CALIFORNIA'S PRISON SYSTEM...
WHO PROFESS TO KNOW THE MURDERER, OR ELSE ADMIT TO THE CRIME THEMSELVES.
BY MARCH, IN FACT, NO FEWER THAN THREE HUNDRED PEOPLE, IN THE UNITED STATES AND ABROAD, HAVE CONFESSED TO THE MURDER OF WILLIAM DESMOND TAYLOR.
THE LOS ANGELES POLICE, DILIGENTLY PURSUING EVERY LEAD, COME TO ONE DEAD END AFTER ANOTHER...
UNTIL AT LAST THE INVESTIGATION SLOWS TO A HALT.

PART VI

AN OPEN CASE

STARS OF THE PHOTOPLAY

LILLIAN GISH

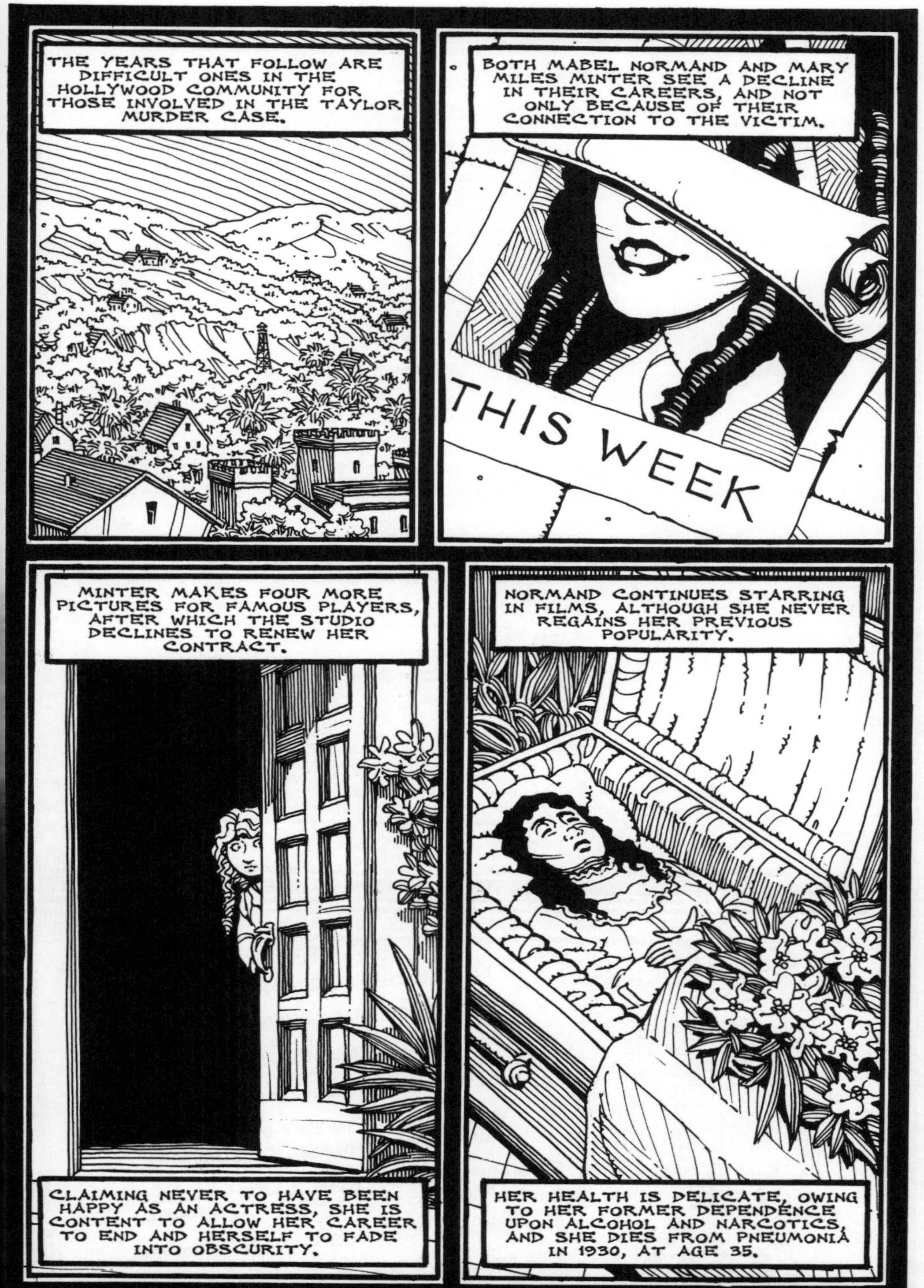
THE YEARS THAT FOLLOW ARE DIFFICULT ONES IN THE HOLLYWOOD COMMUNITY FOR THOSE INVOLVED IN THE TAYLOR MURDER CASE.
BOTH MABEL NORMAND AND MARY MILES MINTER SEE A DECLINE IN THEIR CAREERS, AND NOT ONLY BECAUSE OF THEIR CONNECTION TO THE VICTIM.
THIS WEEK
MINTER MAKES FOUR MORE PICTURES FOR FAMOUS PLAYERS, AFTER WHICH THE STUDIO DECLINES TO RENEW HER CONTRACT.
CLAIMING NEVER TO HAVE BEEN HAPPY AS AN ACTRESS, SHE IS CONTENT TO ALLOW HER CAREER TO END AND HERSELF TO FADE INTO OBSCURITY.
NORMAND CONTINUES STARRING IN FILMS, ALTHOUGH SHE NEVER REGAINS HER PREVIOUS POPULARITY.
HER HEALTH IS DELICATE, OWING TO HER FORMER DEPENDENCE UPON ALCOHOL AND NARCOTICS, AND SHE DIES FROM PNEUMONIA IN 1930, AT AGE 35.

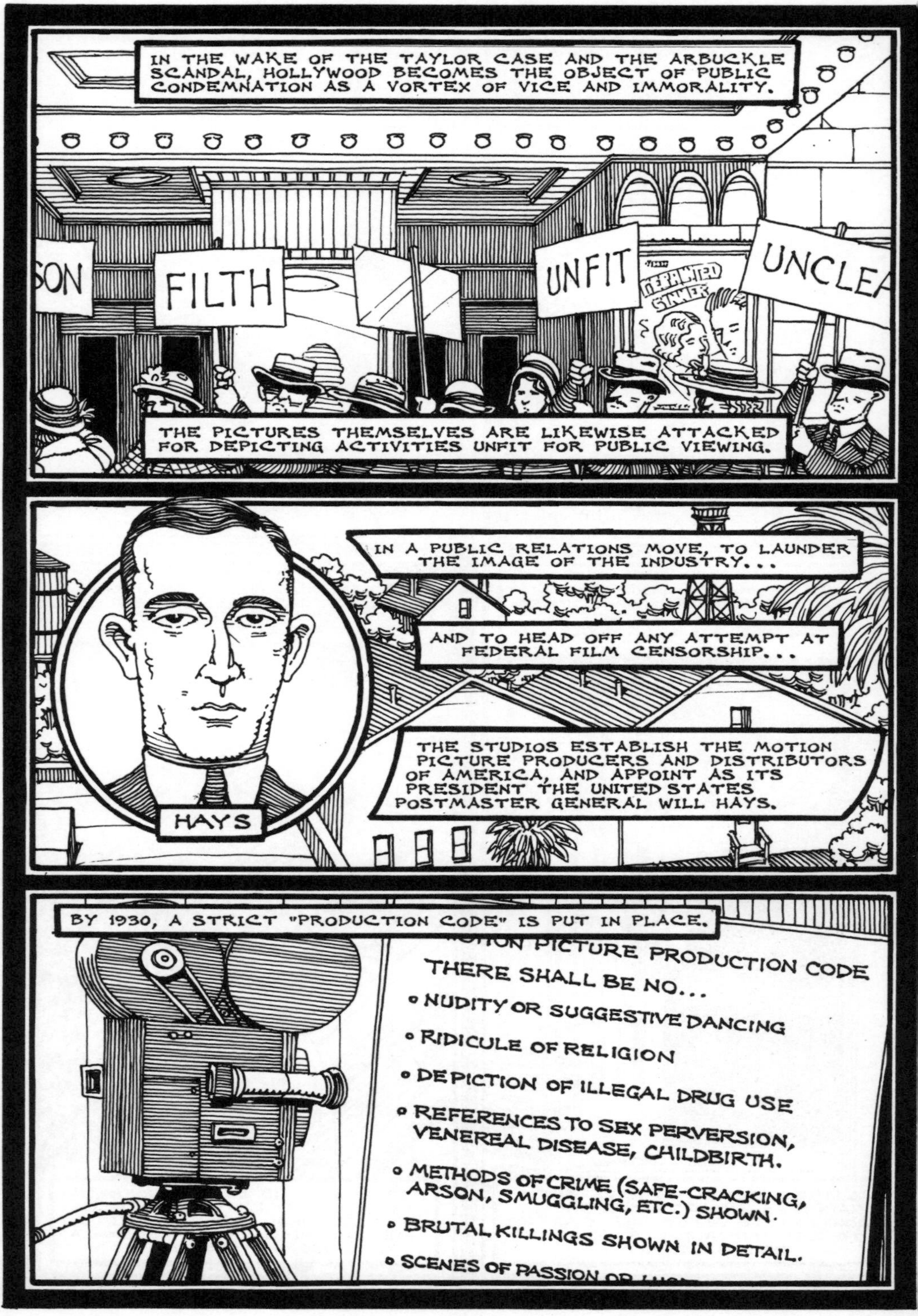
IN THE WAKE OF THE TAYLOR CASE AND THE ARBUCKLE SCANDAL, HOLLYWOOD BECOMES THE OBJECT OF PUBLIC CONDEMNATION AS A VORTEX OF VICE AND IMMORALITY.
FILTH
UNFIT
THE PICTURES THEMSELVES ARE LIKEWISE ATTACKED FOR DEPICTING ACTIVITIES UNFIT FOR PUBLIC VIEWING.
IN A PUBLIC RELATIONS MOVE, TO LAUNDER THE IMAGE OF THE INDUSTRY...
AND TO HEAD OFF ANY ATTEMPT AT FEDERAL FILM CENSORSHIP...
THE STUDIOS ESTABLISH THE MOTION PICTURE PRODUCERS AND DISTRIBUTORS OF AMERICA, AND APPOINT AS ITS PRESIDENT THE UNITED STATES POSTMASTER GENERAL WILL HAYS.
HAYS
BY 1930, A STRICT "PRODUCTION CODE" IS PUT IN PLACE.
PICTURE PRODUCTION CODE
THERE SHALL BE NO...
• NUDITY OR SUGGESTIVE DANCING
• RIDICULE OF RELIGION
• DEPICTION OF ILLEGAL DRUG USE
• REFERENCES TO SEX PERVERSION, VENEREAL DISEASE, CHILDBIRTH.
• METHODS OF CRIME (SAFE-CRACKING, ARSON, SMUGGLING, ETC.) SHOWN.
• BRUTAL KILLINGS SHOWN IN DETAIL.
• SCENES OF PASSION

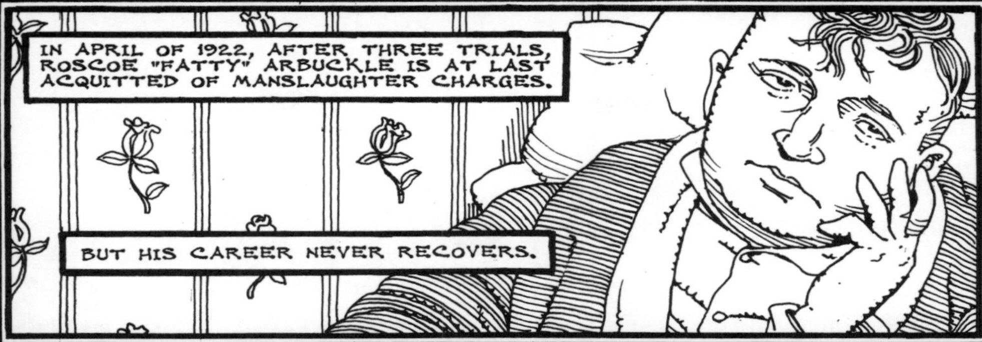
IN APRIL OF 1922, AFTER THREE TRIALS, ROSCOE "FATTY" ARBUCKLE IS AT LAST ACQUITTED OF MANSLAUGHTER CHARGES.
BUT HIS CAREER NEVER RECOVERS.

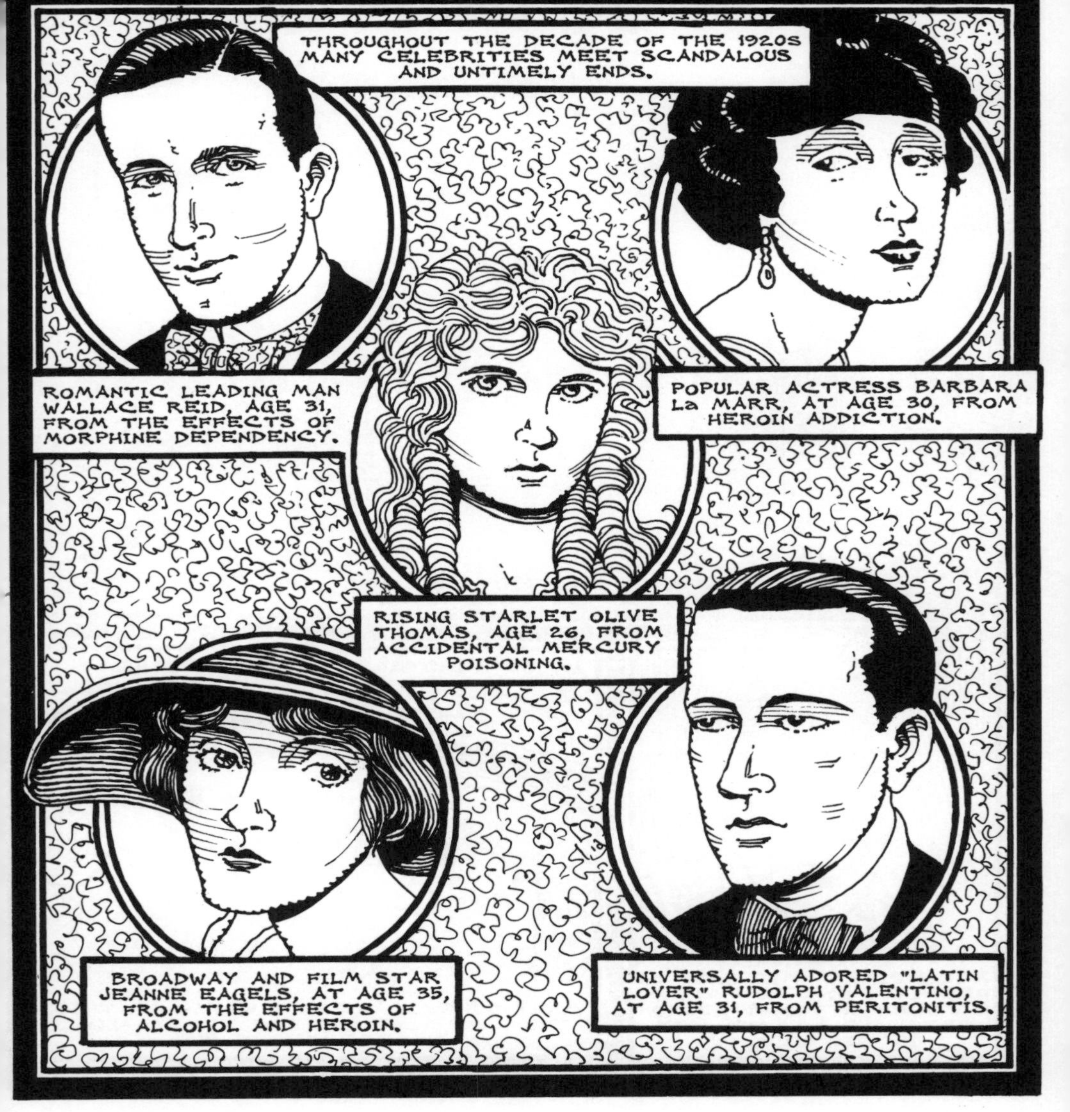
THROUGHOUT THE DECADE OF THE 1920S MANY CELEBRITIES MEET SCANDALOUS AND UNTIMELY ENDS.
ROMANTIC LEADING MAN WALLACE REID, AGE 31, FROM THE EFFECTS OF MORPHINE DEPENDENCY.
POPULAR ACTRESS BARBARA La MARR, AT AGE 30, FROM HEROIN ADDICTION.
RISING STARLET OLIVE THOMAS, AGE 26, FROM ACCIDENTAL MERCURY POISONING.
BROADWAY AND FILM STAR JEANNE EAGELS, AT AGE 35, FROM THE EFFECTS OF ALCOHOL AND HEROIN.
UNIVERSALLY ADORED "LATIN LOVER" RUDOLPH VALENTINO, AT AGE 31, FROM PERITONITIS.

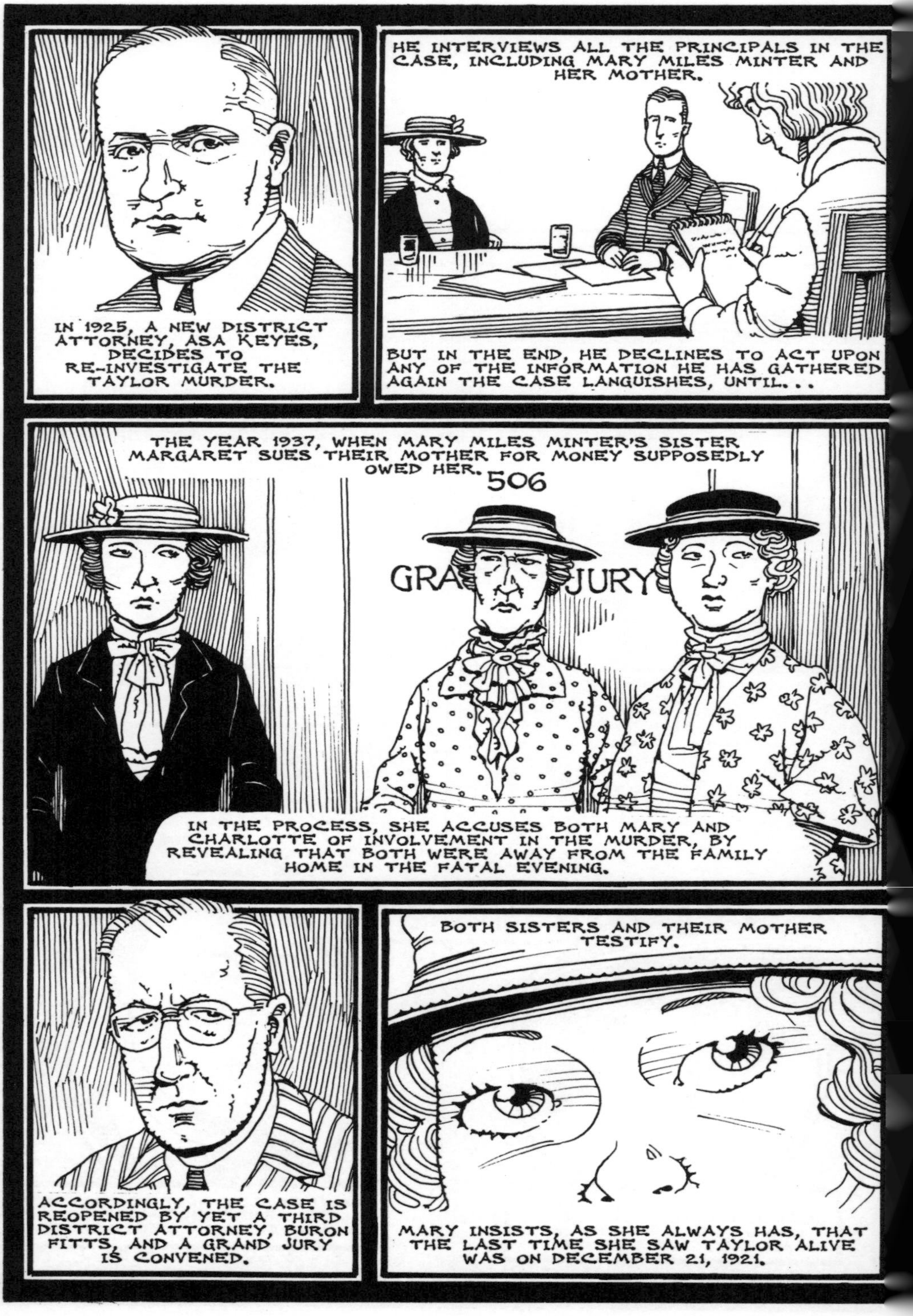
IN 1925, A NEW DISTRICT ATTORNEY, ASA KEYES, DECIDES TO RE-INVESTIGATE THE TAYLOR MURDER.
HE INTERVIEWS ALL THE PRINCIPALS IN THE CASE, INCLUDING MARY MILES MINTER AND HER MOTHER.
BUT IN THE END, HE DECLINES TO ACT UPON ANY OF THE INFORMATION HE HAS GATHERED. AGAIN THE CASE LANGUISHES, UNTIL. . .
THE YEAR 1937, WHEN MARY MILES MINTER'S SISTER MARGARET SUES THEIR MOTHER FOR MONEY SUPPOSEDLY OWED HER.
506
GRA JURY
IN THE PROCESS, SHE ACCUSES BOTH MARY AND CHARLOTTE OF INVOLVEMENT IN THE MURDER, BY REVEALING THAT BOTH WERE AWAY FROM THE FAMILY HOME IN THE FATAL EVENING.
ACCORDINGLY, THE CASE IS REOPENED BY YET A THIRD DISTRICT ATTORNEY, BURON FITTS, AND A GRAND JURY IS CONVENED.
BOTH SISTERS AND THEIR MOTHER TESTIFY.
MARY INSISTS, AS SHE ALWAYS HAS, THAT THE LAST TIME SHE SAW TAYLOR ALIVE WAS ON DECEMBER 21, 1921.

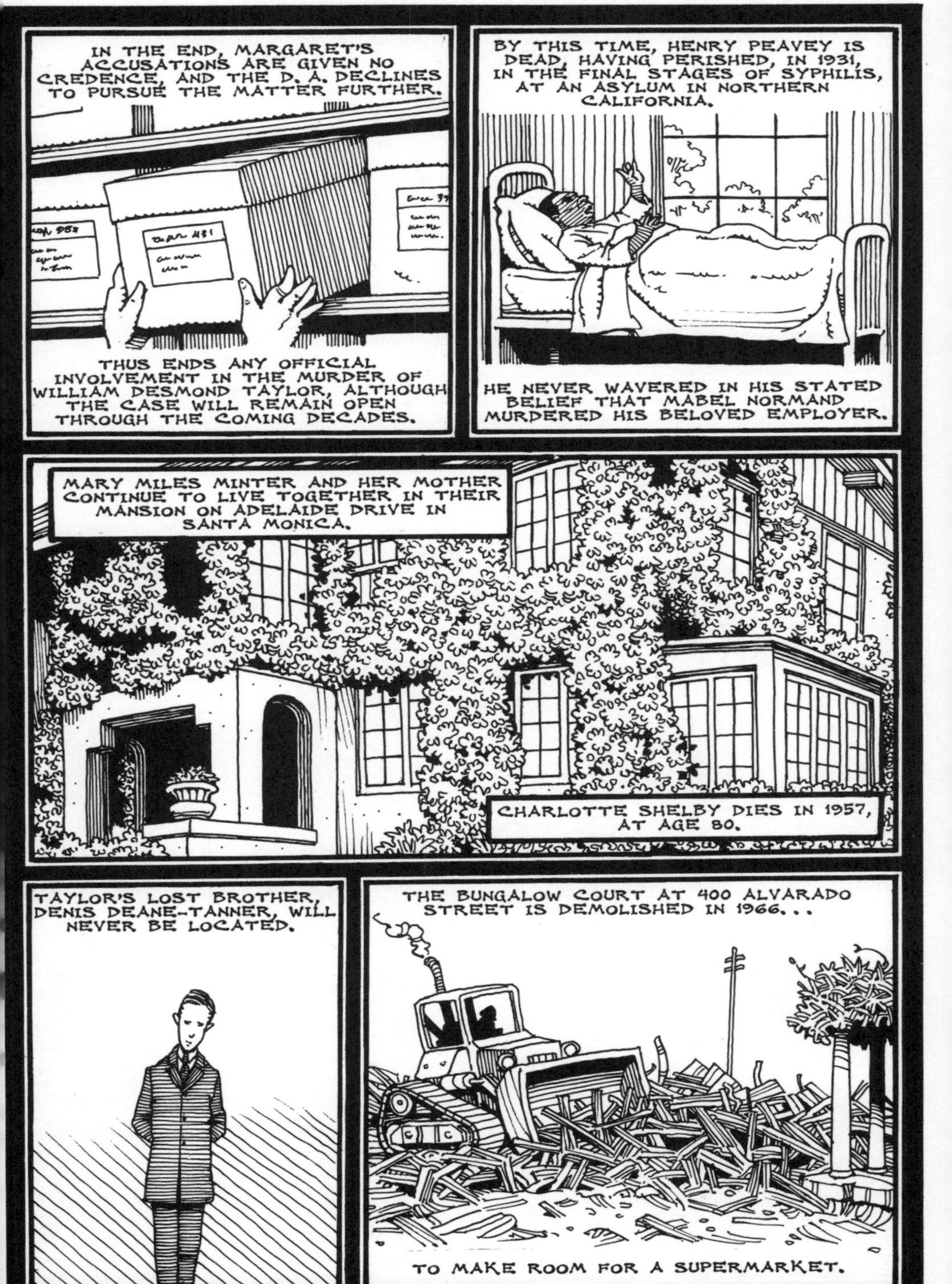
IN THE END, MARGARET'S ACCUSATIONS ARE GIVEN NO CREDENCE, AND THE D. A. DECLINES TO PURSUE THE MATTER FURTHER.
THUS ENDS ANY OFFICIAL INVOLVEMENT IN THE MURDER OF WILLIAM DESMOND TAYLOR, ALTHOUGH THE CASE WILL REMAIN OPEN THROUGH THE COMING DECADES.
BY THIS TIME, HENRY PEAVEY IS DEAD, HAVING PERISHED, IN 1931, IN THE FINAL STAGES OF SYPHILIS, AT AN ASYLUM IN NORTHERN CALIFORNIA.
HE NEVER WAVERED IN HIS STATED BELIEF THAT MABEL NORMAND MURDERED HIS BELOVED EMPLOYER.
MARY MILES MINTER AND HER MOTHER CONTINUE TO LIVE TOGETHER IN THEIR MANSION ON ADELAIDE DRIVE IN SANTA MONICA.
CHARLOTTE SHELBY DIES IN 1957, AT AGE 80.
TAYLOR'S LOST BROTHER, DENIS DEANE-TANNER, WILL NEVER BE LOCATED.
THE BUNGALOW COURT AT 400 ALVARADO STREET IS DEMOLISHED IN 1966. . .
TO MAKE ROOM FOR A SUPERMARKET.

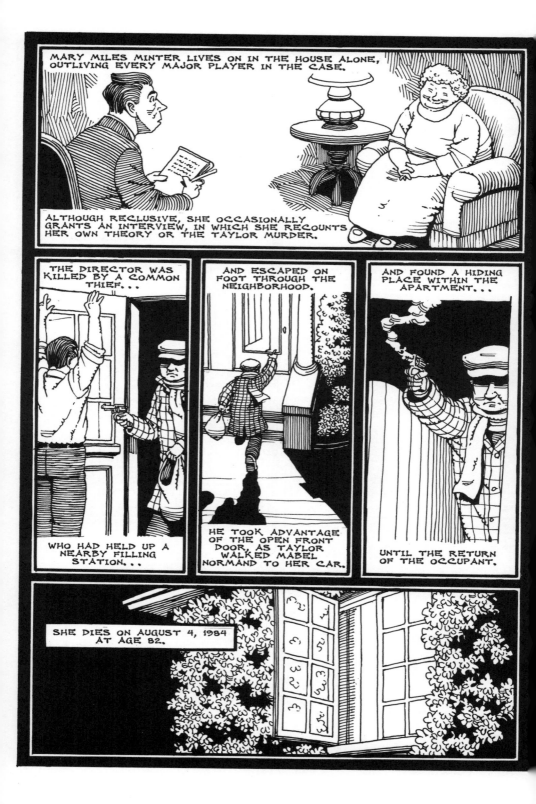

MARY MILES MINTER LIVES ON IN THE HOUSE ALONE, OUTLIVING EVERY MAJOR PLAYER IN THE CASE.

ALTHOUGH RECLUSIVE, SHE OCCASIONALLY GRANTS AN INTERVIEW, IN WHICH SHE RECOUNTS HER OWN THEORY OF THE TAYLOR MURDER.

THE DIRECTOR WAS KILLED BY A COMMON THIEF...

WHO HAD HELD UP A NEARBY FILLING STATION...

AND ESCAPED ON FOOT THROUGH THE NEIGHBORHOOD.

HE TOOK ADVANTAGE OF THE OPEN FRONT DOOR, AS TAYLOR WALKED MABEL NORMAND TO HER CAR.

AND FOUND A HIDING PLACE WITHIN THE APARTMENT...

UNTIL THE RETURN OF THE OCCUPANT.

SHE DIES ON AUGUST 4, 1984 AT AGE 82.

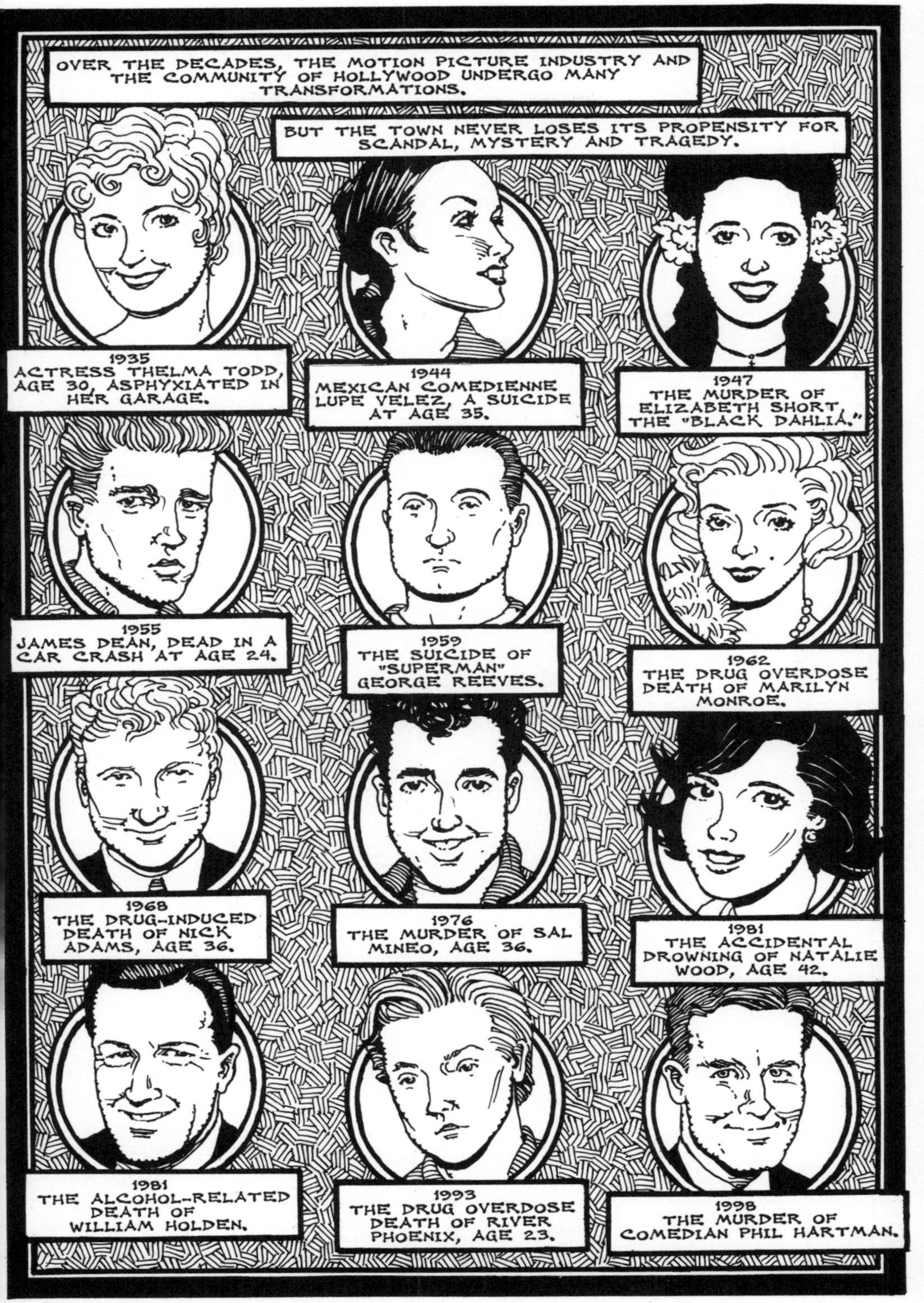
OVER THE DECADES, THE MOTION PICTURE INDUSTRY AND THE COMMUNITY OF HOLLYWOOD UNDERGO MANY TRANSFORMATIONS.
BUT THE TOWN NEVER LOSES ITS PROPENSITY FOR SCANDAL, MYSTERY AND TRAGEDY.
1935 ACTRESS THELMA TODD, AGE 30, ASPHYXIATED IN HER GARAGE.
1944 MEXICAN COMEDIENNE LUPE VELEZ, A SUICIDE AT AGE 35.
1947 THE MURDER OF ELIZABETH SHORT, THE "BLACK DAHLIA."
1955 JAMES DEAN, DEAD IN A CAR CRASH AT AGE 24.
1959 THE SUICIDE OF "SUPERMAN" GEORGE REEVES.
1962 THE DRUG OVERDOSE DEATH OF MARILYN MONROE.
1968 THE DRUG-INDUCED DEATH OF NICK ADAMS, AGE 36.
1976 THE MURDER OF SAL MINEO, AGE 36.
1981 THE ACCIDENTAL DROWNING OF NATALIE WOOD, AGE 42.
1981 THE ALCOHOL-RELATED DEATH OF WILLIAM HOLDEN.
1993 THE DRUG OVERDOSE DEATH OF RIVER PHOENIX, AGE 23.
1998 THE MURDER OF COMEDIAN PHIL HARTMAN.

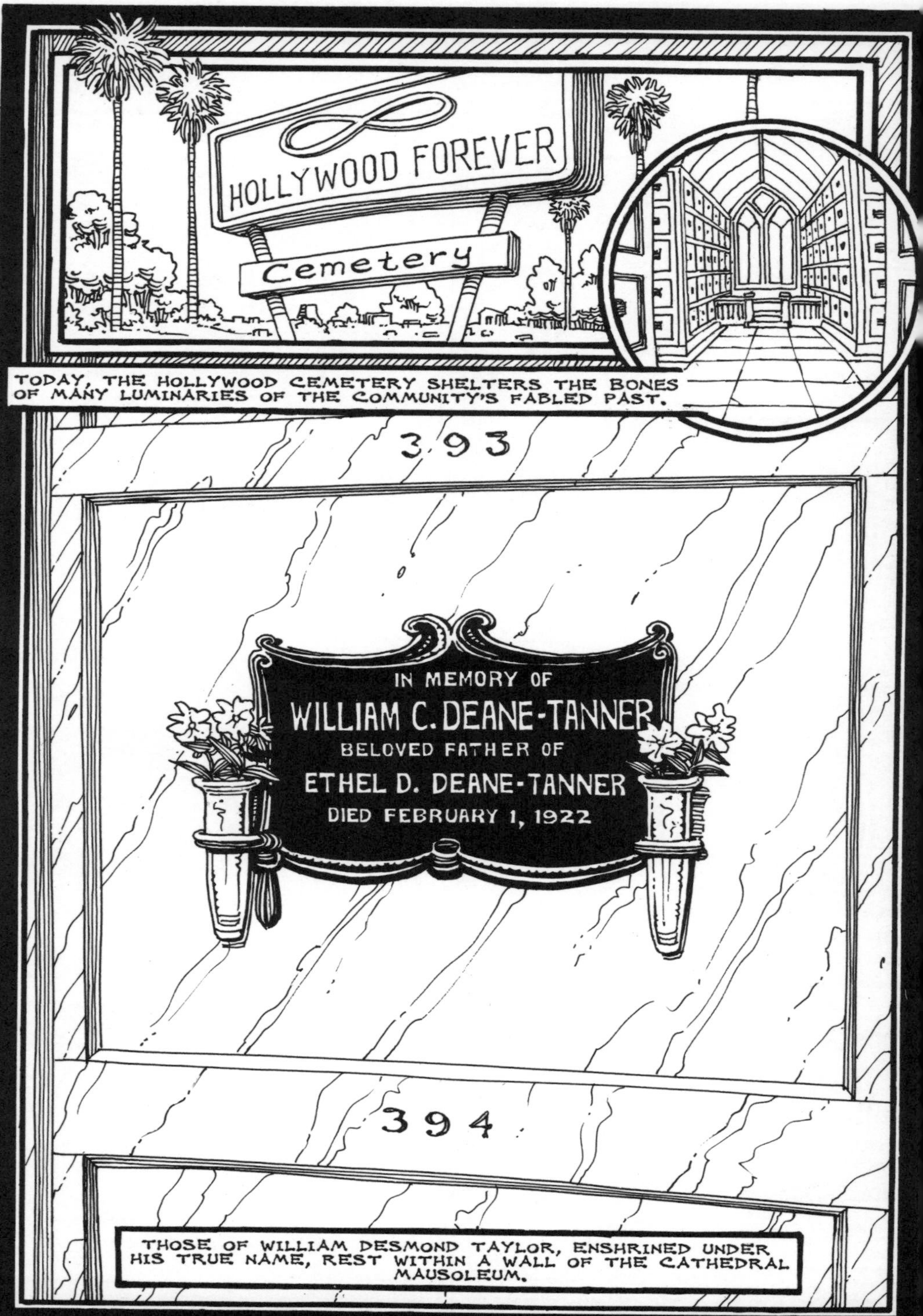
HOLLYWOOD FOREVER
Cemetery
TODAY, THE HOLLYWOOD CEMETERY SHELTERS THE BONES OF MANY LUMINARIES OF THE COMMUNITY'S FABLED PAST.
393
IN MEMORY OF
WILLIAM C. DEANE-TANNER
BELOVED FATHER OF
ETHEL D. DEANE-TANNER
DIED FEBRUARY 1, 1922
394
THOSE OF WILLIAM DESMOND TAYLOR, ENSHRINED UNDER HIS TRUE NAME, REST WITHIN A WALL OF THE CATHEDRAL MAUSOLEUM.